When Sh*t Goes Sideways
Soul-Centered Navigation for Life

Jeanine Tripodi

FIVE
ROOTS
PRESS

Jeanine Tripodi

Cover Photo: Jared Seger Photography

DEDICATION

For my children, Simone, Max, Matilda,
Lola and Rocco.
Thank you for choosing me.

And for my parents, John and Wilma,
who always support me, no matter what.

Jeanine Tripodi

CONTENTS

Jeanine Tripodi

I'M A SOUL SEARCHING ENERGY HEAVY

I thrive on it.

I'm connected with it.

Because I know that this invisible, palpable energy is what connects us all to each other and to ourselves. We are infinite, and we are in constant motion and transition. I love going deep, fast. Small talk is my kryptonite. In a room full of strangers, I'm scanning for vibrations, seeking out the ones who emote. Those deep soul connections, they anchor me. They fill me.

I believe the purpose of life is to experience joy: pure, in the present moment, joy. And I think we get there through our own inner compass, through relationships, and through nature. We're here to guide each other to find more.

I believe the Universe conspires for us,
but that doesn't mean we get to
skip out on the pain.

As a child, I used to stretch an invisible ball between my hands like it was taffy, feeling the outer limits of the sphere and its gentle resistance. I didn't know why I could feel it or really what it was, but I knew it was real. As I played with the energy, I understood my nonphysical world.

My intuition and my connection were strong and natural, but things like that weren't talked about much, so I often kept my experiences to myself. I spent many years shutting down my connection as I focused on the physical and practical.

While I maintained my inner compass, I often needed multiple hits from the Universe to accept messages. That all changed when my son died. That day in the hospital, I had a connection so clear and so loud, I couldn't deny it or doubt it.

It was during that season, deep in my grief, that I was introduced to Reiki. Through that energy work, the darkness cracked open and the light seeped in. When everything was peeled away, I saw what truly mattered in life. I reconnected with the me I've always been.

When my world was dark, I often asked myself, "What is the purpose of life?" Every time, even before I could finish my question, I would hear the answer, "Joy." I believe it's our job to live in joy, to help others find joy, and to spread the love.

Jeanine Tripodi

HOW IT ALL BEGAN

Great things are often born out of necessity. And we all need this.

It isn't about achieving a life without conflict; it's about finding the joy within the chaos and trusting yourself to stay the course.

Also, some days are shit.
This is gonna help.

The Universe offers lessons to give us opportunities to grow. Some lessons are more fun than others, and some are easier. There's no guarantee you're gonna feel ready or willing to take the course. You get to decide — free will and all that.

But you can bet the lessons will keep showing up in different forms until you choose to take notice and get to work. Maybe today, maybe next week, or maybe next life. Anyway, it's sort of like a rope bridge stretched over a bottomless crevasse: you have to cross the bridge because going around is not an option.

I am often surprised by the number of times I get to revisit that rope bridge. It's like, on some whacked-out soul level, I want to test the strength of the ropes again and again and again. Some lessons are just big like that.

Trusting myself and my intuition above the logic of those around me has been a big lesson for me. Today, I am comfortable making some pretty big decisions based on feelings alone. That freaks a lot of people out, especially in my inner circle. Sure, facts and analysis are important, but there is no better measure than your gut feeling. Historically, my intuition is spot-on, even when I look insane to outsiders:

Don't take the job.
(But they're doubling your salary!)

Take that chance.
(There's no proof! It's too risky!)

Don't take that offer.
(They have cash. You're crazy.)

That buddy of yours? He isn't safe.
(He's OK. I've known him for years.)

I went against my inner knowing, and I took that job. It sucked out my soul and left me with thyroid masses. That chance? It worked out better than I could have imagined. The offer? We took it because we needed the cash. They were horrible and cost us more money than I care to admit. That friend's buddy? He tried to rape her.

Over the years, I've had many opportunities to learn to lean in and trust myself, to stay the course, even when the ground shakes. Just when I thought I had passed that test, this lesson showed up for me again, a little differently, and in the middle of developing this program.

In retrospect, it's laughable and also not surprising, that this lesson would come up in my life at the very moment I was defining the problems this program would help people navigate.

At this moment, my husband called to drop two bombs: his photo job, one that would have kept him busy for a month, had been put on hold indefinitely. In addition, a long-term investment, where we thought we'd see promising growth within a month, now looked dismal.

This sent him into a downward spiral; I could hear it in his voice. Then I felt the slow roll of panic build inside me. It was as if the Universe wanted to be sure I tapped back into those feelings I've had so many times before.

It felt like a mirror had been shoved so close to my face, I could feel the heat of my own breath. I had experienced this many times before, yet I still flinched, ready to run, ready to freeze and grasp for solutions from others.

Ten minutes earlier, I had been full of strength and light, beaming with purpose as I sketched on the whiteboard the last bits to be included in the first draft of this book. And then—poof. Fissures and cracks opened up in my subtle energy body, and the light rushed out. My body physically responded, closing in on itself: deflated.

I felt myself begin to step out onto that familiar path I'd taken so many times before when shit went sideways. Stop. Re-pivot. Desperately search for answers outside myself. Frantically put the fire out. My perspective narrowed; I focused on fear.

"I'll pause the program, shut down production. I'll rework my marketing résumé.

I'll . . ."

And then as quickly as the panic rose, an overwhelming wave of calm washed over me. This was my lesson. And this time I was ready.

I knew with every part of me that pressing pause was not the answer. *Butterflies.* I needed to push ahead even harder and stay the course. *Inner knowing.* I needed to trust myself in this moment of fear. My plan hadn't changed; some shit just went sideways. I needed to choose a different response, a different path.

I needed this guide.

And so I finished creating *Soul-Centered Navigation for Life* and the Seven Secrets to Survival *When Sh*t Goes Sideways* because it inevitably does. The chaos is real. And through it all, I want you to remember that guidance, joy, purpose, and direction all come from within.

Jeanine Tripodi

AUTOPILOT

One minute you're racing down the Autobahn, and the next you let go of the wheel.

When shit goes sideways in life, most of us tend to shift into autopilot. Consciously or not, we flip off our connections with ourselves and our intuition. First, trust in our own perspective is shaken, as if this external disruption creates a tidal wave washing away faith in ourselves.

We lose purpose. We forget that we are driven from the power within. Doubt creeps in, and we lose sight of joy. We hand off the wheel to others, and we start scanning outside of ourselves for validation, security, happiness, purpose, and direction.

When the flow of life is disrupted, it's in our nature to close off, to narrow our focus, but our eyes often land on fear. Some frantically grasp for quick solutions anywhere, like casting the net wide and shallow, skimming just the surface. But the truth is, when you fish like this, you only catch the chum — or maybe not even that, honestly, I don't know. Does chum float? You only catch the surface crap.

You get the idea. The ground feels shaky. Plans start to feel weak. More doubt and vulnerability set in. The ego starts to sweat, and so it reaches for reassurance.

Our instinct is to contract when we should expand.

This is the rhythm for so many of us, and it's backward.

Trust me on this. Stay strong, dive in, ask yourself first because you have the answers inside. Inside, you'll find peace. Chaos exists all around us. We weave it into the web of static we as humans innately create. It's the search for joy within the chaos that tests our fortitude.

Why is the instinct to abandon self and reach outside of ourselves for answers and validation? It's in this moment that it's most urgent to listen to your soul's voice. This is the time to dig deep, tap in, trust your connection to the Universe, and lead with your heart.

The chaos may still exist, but your experience of it will change, and so will the way you navigate out. My Seven Secrets to Survival When Shit Goes Sideways will teach you to shift from fear, panic, and uncertainty to calm, peace, and possibility. Only from that place can we clearly see opportunities for change. Life rafts head for shore. When you lean in and trust yourself, especially when it's scary, you will thrive, even when shit goes sideways.

Jeanine Tripodi

The Intention

The intention of the secrets to survival When Sh*t Goes Sideways is to nudge you on a path where:

- You remember your connection to your higher Self, the Universe, and each other;

- You feel guided by your own purpose;

- You mine your own soul for solutions instead of allowing the external noise to dictate your goals, next steps, and measures of success;

- You remember the feeling of being whole, connected, joyful, and enough;

- You trust your intuition, inner knowing, and own connection above all else;

- You move forward and find joy within the chaos;

- You validate your mystical experiences;

- You drive life from your heart;

- You know you are not alone; and

- You hear and trust your soul's voice.

So go all in. I do. In this book, I set out to bring you into my world, while helping you shine your light on your own. I've naturally been one to find the cracks of light, even in the darkness. Sure, it has not always been in the exact moment when life feels like it's crumbling, but it happens somewhere along the path back home. In these pages, I share some light stories that I hope will make you laugh, but I also want to bring you deep into some of my heavy, Universe-tilting losses. I share this all with love and the wish that you will see yourself in these stories, you will remember your inner wisdom, and you'll find your own joy.

Use this book to reconnect with all the parts of you and to expand your views and understanding of your physical and nonphysical worlds. These exercises and reflections will encourage you to be your own guru, your own guide, and your own touchstone. They will also remind you that we are born into families and communities and that we thrive with dynamic and healthy relationships. We are stronger together. Lean on each other but drive from a place within. We are here to raise our frequency together, to share the lessons, love, and joy. We are here to support each other.

As you explore these concepts and secrets, linger as long as you'd like. Mull them over. Make notes. Come back to these ideas and apply them to your experiences. This kind of journey changes and becomes more faceted as your life experience and understanding changes. Return to sections and cull deeper for more insight.

My understanding of the secrets grows each year. The beauty of this kind of work is that it continues to expand with you. Review notes over time. Appreciate where you've seen more freedom and growth, and notice which ideas you want to revisit.

Soul-centered navigation unfolds in new ways as you begin to see things from different perspectives. That's why I made a workbook available. You can come back to the secrets with fresh eyes and a new page when life takes a turn. The workbooks are available individually and in a three-pack because, if you're like me, you'll want to rework the secrets throughout the year. Put them into practice when you embark on a life change or when life rolls out an unexpected lesson. Do it your way. Be open to doing it new ways. Trust your Self.

Navigate with friends because expansion and freedom love community. Collect your tribe and start a book club. Sharing insights with a trusted group of friends raises everyone's vibrations.

So, pull out your *When Sh*t Goes Sideways Workbook* or if you're using a blank journal or paper, jot down the Soul Centers below.

Soul Centers are areas of life. Throughout several of this book's *Exercises & Reflections* you will be asked to reflect on each area of life.

Tribe

Body

Soul

Tribe encompasses relationships and how you connect with others. This includes family, a significant other, children, friends, associates, second-tier circles of your tribe, and work/career relationships. Tribe may also include your relationship with work, career, or religion as a whole. In other words, Tribe refers to your interpersonal relationships, as well as your relationship with institutions of work and religion.

Body encompasses your physical body, health, and wellness. The physical, grounded humanness.

Soul encompasses your higher Self, spirituality, your passion(s), joy, and creativity.

One last note before you dive in, you will notice I separate *Self* from *yourself* throughout this book. I do this intentionally to remind you to bring awareness beyond your physical self to your higher Self. And your higher Self deserves a capital "S," as it is your direct connection to the divine and the Universe as you know it. The Universe is also capitalized, as my use of the word expands beyond the stars and galaxy to include a higher power — whatever your understanding of that may be.

For ongoing connection to the larger tribe, join us at JeanineTripodi.com/WSGS

Jeanine Tripodi

Chapter 1

Jeanine Tripodi

Secret #1:
The Humanness of Chaos

I turn to flush the toilet in the master, and the handle clinks: zero resistance. It just stands there completely fucking vertical. That's not right. We are already down one toilet in a house full of six people.

A subtle, early-morning reminder
that chaos still breeds.

Before I get out of bed each morning, I put my hands over my heart and tap in. I ask my guides, "What is it that I need to see, hear, feel, or know right now?" Then I listen for that first inner reply, and I trust it. This practice brings me peace. It makes me feel better, and it reminds me to drive my choices from the heart. It's poetic, really, this gentle flow to life, confident that the answers will come. I know that direction and purpose come from within. I share this with my clients, helping them to find balance and trust their connection to the Universe. I love connecting with people's energy and delivering the messages I pick up from the spirit. I know it's what I came here to do. I know it deep in my soul. It's magical. But I'm not gonna lie: some days are shit.

We have always had a way of deceiving the public, unintentionally. It must be that my husband, Jared, and I really do love life, and we look happy more often than not. We live in a beautiful home in a suburb with wonderful neighbors, a pool, and four kids who are nearly always laughing and playing. Jared works from home as a photographer, and his work is outstanding. People follow his Instagram and see images of his travel and adventures.

What they don't know is that nearly $100,000 in medical bills plus a failed business investment will really fuck up your perfect credit. God damn, I had perfect credit for forty-six years. My biggest financial fear was actualized: bankruptcy. My daughter has anxiety that manifests as facial tics and circular thoughts. Her twin hates to read. The kids' toilet has been broken for a year, so...*toothpaste all over my bath towel.* My husband is a recovering alcoholic. The dog died a week before Christmas. It's my fault we sold our idyllic Oregon farm and moved to the desert. And twelve years ago, our son, Max, died.

There's more, but you get the point. We all have issues. I used to worry that having issues while helping others meant that I was a fraud. I gave up that kind of thinking years ago. I now know it means that we are human. I have been wanting to write this program for a decade, but I was sort of waiting for life to smooth out first. I recently realized that this may be the whole point.

> *It isn't about achieving a life without conflict; it's about staying the course during the chaos.*

It's about tapping into ourselves and trusting our connection with our higher Selves and with our guides and angels. It's about more than being human. It's about our connection between the physical and the nonphysical and how, when we really live, we live in between.

Some days, I struggle to stay aligned with my core truths. Don't get me wrong, I am a strong woman, and I navigate the shit out of life changes, but some days I am surprised to find that even though I am a badass full of self-help skills, my life often tries to unfold guided by autopilot and driven by external input and expectation. These are the days I remind myself that I am guided by my own purpose. I trust myself and my connection to the Universe above all else, and I try to find joy within the chaos even when shit goes sideways. You see, I'm not just talking the talk, I'm actually a student of the Secrets.

We live in a fast-paced, information-streaming society, and those streams flow increasingly faster. I try to avoid my phone until after I have had my coffee and meditation, or I can be quickly sucked into headlines, posts, and greener grass imagery, only to be bitch slapped by the latest crisis, political lie, failing system, or custom-filtered image of the life I suddenly think I want—no, need.

Contrary to what the impossibly flawless model on the magazine cover says and the promises made by that new product we all just must have, the truth is if you can't find joy despite your circumstances, no circumstance will bring you joy. Realizing what your soul really wants and needs is the key to Joy with a capital "J." Maintaining the focus on your core truths in the midst of the chaos is the key to freedom.

Social media has done some amazing things for our world. Growing up in the seventies, we had to wait for the hippie from Greenpeace to knock on our front door so we could hand over our babysitting money to save the whales. Now you can launch your own birthday fundraiser to hundreds of friends with the click of a button. As good as it is, it has also stripped us of reality in so many ways. It has rewritten the expectations that we create for ourselves and for others. Life isn't flawless.

The chaos is real. Toilets break. We have kids and partners and friends in crisis. We have plans that went left when we were still tracking right. We are faced with decisions we never imagined making. We stand teetering in heels, grasping at ideals that we fed in the hope of becoming that person. We listened too much to the outside noises and not enough to the voices in our head, and we shifted into autopilot before we even realized our hands were off the wheel. It's all part of being human.

As you think about your life circumstances right now, whether you are feeling deep sadness or fear or grief or ambivalence, remember that no matter what is or has transpired, it has brought you here. In this moment you have the power to choose. Choose to tap in and take inspired action. Choose joy in the midst of chaos because we all need to remember the feeling of joy. Choose to recalibrate your energy and launch yourself in a more soul-inspired direction. Choose to lean in and step beyond the fear.

Don't waste time with should-haves and what-ifs. Regardless of what has brought you here, YOU are the sum of all of your parts, even the painful ones. There is light around the corner, I promise. You just need to take the steps. There is a saying, "Hope without action is a waste of fucking energy and time." Nah, that's probably not exactly right, but you get it.

We all make mistakes. We all choose poorly at times, and the road to perfection isn't paved. Also, it doesn't exist. So, maybe stop trying to find it? Dwell in the dark caves of pain for a few moments, but be ready to navigate out after you've looked around a bit. Feeling unsettled, scared, insecure, cheated, or sorrowful is a temporary stop on the trail of life. It's not a place to set up camp. Shit goes sideways, chaos happens, and when you can accept that this is all a part of life, the journey is less scary, and the idea of getting through feels more real because it is.

No one is immune to chaos.

Lose denial and accept that this is real. The Universe offers lessons and opportunities for us to dive deeply into experiences so that, should we choose, we can learn and share from our hearts.

Because of this, it is no surprise that as I type my manuscript, life as I know it feels like I'm teetering on a sinking iceberg—well, maybe not sinking so much as changing to an unrecognizable landscape. The chaos, buried for a time, reemerges when life throws us off course. We slide into miscommunications and outright lies and land in the treacherous waters of not trusting what once felt reliable.

I've lost sleep. I've lost weight. I've felt thick, suffocating fear, and I have asked myself, "What am I supposed to do?" The only thing that has brought me any clarity and peace is re-reading this manuscript. And so I breathe. I accept the chaos, find my universe, tap in, tell better stories, gather my tools, ask for help, and choose joy.

Trust

your *Self*

above all else.

More often than not, we try to outrun the chaos, ignore it, or search for a life without it.

Avoiding these inevitable parts of life cheapens the very experience of joy. After Max died, I asked the group counselor if I would ever feel joy again. I was sure her shoulders would drop as she prepared me for a life of dulled emotions and dark corners of sadness. Instead, she took a breath and quietly said, "I have been told you'll feel joy in more vibrant ways than you could ever have before."

She was right. The effect of experiencing the full spectrum of heartbreak somehow awakened a more colorful palette. I was shown hues of emotion that never before existed for me on earth. It took some time, no doubt. And I would never have chosen this path, but since I cannot change the past, I choose to be grateful for the access to the enhanced spectrum of joy. If I hadn't accepted the chaos, I might have missed the joy.

Accepting that the chaos is real is freeing. Accepting the humanness of chaos allows us to stand firm in our story, and from that point, pivot from the heart. When we accept, we let go of the nagging pressure to compare our lives and situations to others. We let go of the need to resist, and we have all heard that what we resist persists. Accepting the humanness of chaos reminds us that we are enough, that life is supposed to be a hot mess, and that there is beauty in the chaos.

Beyond question, the meaning of life is to find JOY and to share it with others. As you read through these Secrets, just remember, joy doesn't wait for us around the corner from the chaos. Joy lives within us even when the chaos teems.

Your chaos is real, and it's a part of life. Swallow that bitter pill, chase it with some Häagen-Dazs, and move on to the exercises and reflections.

It's no secret: Acceptance is the first step in shifting perspective. You're here, which means you are already recalibrating.

Exercises & Reflections:

It's time to pull out your *When Sh*t Goes Sideways* Workbook or if you're using a blank journal or paper, jot down the Soul Centers; *Tribe, Body, and Soul.*

If you aren't clear on what Soul Centers are, you can jump back to *The Intention* section for a quick review.

Accepting that the chaos is real is more than simply agreeing you've got chaos in your life. It's about acknowledging the chaos, identifying how it shows up, and determining how and if you want to reprogram your automatic responses.

These responses are developed by the subconscious mind. Your subconscious mind records everything that you do, experience, and feel, and then it creates patterns for future use. This serves you well when you have effective patterns, however, it can keep you stuck if those responses are less than ideal.

You already have many programmed patterns that you access in response to chaos. Let's take a look at them, evaluate them, and modify them, if needed.

1) *Reflecting on each Soul Center, where does chaos currently show up? Describe it.*

Journal your responses. This may take just a few

minutes, or you might want to sit with this a while. This is where the work begins. Don't rush it. Be vulnerable. It doesn't need to make sense to anyone else. Review all Soul Centers and allow yourself to release the words onto the page.

2) *What does chaos feel like?*

Go back through each example above and evaluate how you feel when experiencing the chaos. Where does it show up in your body? Does your heart race? Do you feel heaviness in your gut? Do you have a difficult time thinking clearly? Get specific about how it *feels*.

3) *What is your first response to each example of chaos?*

Do you shut down, do you lean in, do you give in, do you say "No," do you get fired up? Don't let your ego get caught up in this response. Visualize being in the example you described above and relive the first moments. What did you do, feel or say?

4) *Identify patterns.* Now re-read your examples of chaos, where they show up in your life, how they feel to you and what your first response is. Look for patterns.

5) *Reevaluate your responses.* You've looked at your automatic response to chaos, is this how you'd like to respond? If yes, awesome, you're more evolved than most! If no, how would you like to shift your response? Would you prefer to greet chaos with calm and the knowing that you can navigate out? Would you like to be clearheaded and ready to calculate your next move?

6) *How are you going to shift your responses?* Now that you have identified how you'd like to respond, list some ways to help yourself get there. This may include creating exercises to do in the moment, a brief visualization to calm and ground yourself, or a memory of a time when chaos struck and you navigated out smoothly.

7) *Create your new mantra for chaos.* Start with the feelings. We want to go beneath the surface of the chaotic event and identify the feeling before it triggers your programmed response.

For each example you have identified write:

When chaos strikes and I feel _____ *I will* _____.

Chapter 2

Jeanine Tripodi

Secret #2:
Find Your Universe

This is a big one. I'm asking you to stretch your thinking and explode past the edges of your current understanding. Fracture the limits of your existing beliefs and tell yourself what you feel is true to you, not what you've been taught is true.

Whether we remember our experiences consciously or not, reality can be shadowed by expectations of our culture. Journal. Re-read your own words when doubt creeps in. I share a lot in this section because, in my experience, hearing other people's stories, especially when parts resonate even just a little, validates that you aren't alone and can give you permission to step into the possibility that life is more than what we see in front of us every day.

Have you ever asked yourself how life works?

I don't mean that drunken, "What the hell is life about anyway?!" sort of asking. I mean have you really ever taken the time to wonder, what is Life? Does it end when this body stops? Are we all walking our own paths alone? Or is there something greater that connects us? I used to wonder this a lot.

It never made sense to me that this would be "it." But I also couldn't wrap my head around the stories traditional doctrines told. Granted, I had limited understanding of them. My parents let us decide whether we wanted to attend church or not. Frankly, when choosing between getting dressed up to sit through church service or eating cereal in my jammies while watching *Tom & Jerry*, the cat and mouse seemed like the logical choice. But just in case God didn't approve of my decision, I also tuned into the *Davey and Goliath* cartoon too. I felt like I was covering my bases, and, anyway, the times I had been in church felt scary. The imagery was unsettling to me. What others saw as beautiful, I saw as frightening and painful and sorrowful. The priest's voice echoed and reverberated in my throat. I felt isolated and alone. I wanted to talk to God directly, but I was told that wasn't allowed; I had to go through the priest. That made no sense to me. Why, if we were all children of God, couldn't we have a direct line? I'm not trying to argue the ways of the Catholic Church, I'm just saying, even as a child, some of the rules felt manmade.

I much preferred to see the world through nature. I was fascinated with stories of the ways Native Americans lived at one with nature and with animals, enthralled by the idea that everything had a spirit.

My father has always been a wonderful storyteller. He can recall dates, times, names, and details with the accuracy of a historian. I can't recall the name of my favorite song or the author of the book I'm reading. But my dad, he can spin tales with such detail and emotion that at times I am able to feel what it was like to live in that time or that place. I used to love going on long car rides with him because it was like having my very own historical orator. He could bring alive the driest of history. And when we talked about religion or God or the Universe, my parents always asked what I thought was the truth. They never told me to blindly believe in another's vision. Of all of the gifts they have given me, I do believe this may be the greatest.

They gave me permission to listen to the Universe, to hear it speak to me directly, to decipher its meaning as only I could understand. And I listened.

I was about nine the first time I remember the Universe talking to me. I was sitting on my bed. I was supposed to be asleep, but I was wide awake and very bored. My grandpa Tripodi had recently died, and from my bed I could see his photo hanging on the wall in the hallway. I would look over at it and tell him I loved him. I could feel this connection with him as if a dark, thick line or rope extended from my heart to him through this photo.

"Can you hear me, Grandpa?" I asked.

I knew the answer was yes before I even completed my thought, but I finished asking anyway. I had looked at that photo dozens of times, sending him love and smiles, but on this particular night, as I asked him, I saw his eyes squint in a smile. He moved. Legit, moved. In that moment, I had a rush of memories of his smell, his smile, and the way his temple pulsed when he ate asparagus out of the boat-shaped dish that Grandma Tripodi gave just to him. I remembered that time we rode the T in Boston to the ice-cream parlor and how that boy jumped up to give my grandfather the only seat in the entire shop. It was an old school desk, so out of place.

I blinked super wide, trying to clear my eyes. I freaked. I immediately asked him not to see me through the picture, and the photo felt empty again. You see, that's how it works. When you ask, they listen. I never saw the photo move again. In fact, I don't think I felt him again until twenty-six years later.

They say there are times in our lives when we are more open to connecting with the Universe. Puberty, for example, is a common time for people to experience psychic awareness. That was the beginning of one of those times for me.

It was there, sitting up in bed at night, that I discovered the subtle energy of chi and my etheric field. I don't even know how it started, but I was trying to pass the time and began tapping my fingertips together, then tapping my palms together, first fast, then slow. Then I pretended I had taffy in my hands. I felt a resistance! I gasped and tried it again. Nothing: but I knew it was real. I didn't know how to explain it, but I felt it. It was like two opposing magnets in my palms.

I tried again, moving my hands slowly. I stared at the space between my palms until my gaze softened and the air thickened. There it was. I could feel this ball between my hands. I explored the edges of the ball, slowly moving my hands around as if I held an invisible sphere. It was amazing.

But every time I thought about it, every time I focused on the fact that I could feel something that I could not see, I lost it. Again I would softened my gaze and slowly bring my palms together, and again I would find the sphere. Playing with this ball of energy I learned that if I moved my hands too quickly, I lost it. If I questioned it, I lost it.

I wondered if I should share this with anyone else.

No. How would I explain?

There were a lot of things I didn't understand and a lot of things I couldn't explain.

One day after Grandpa died, we were visiting my grandmother at her apartment in Boston. I loved going into the city to visit her. We lived in a saltbox house in the suburbs, so exploring her old apartment was magical: the old-fashioned push-button light switches, the cracking plaster walls, all the little details in the trim, and the ornate doorknobs. I was certain that one day I would find a real jewel hiding and long forgotten in one of those knobs.

When you walked through the front door, there was a formal sitting room to the left. In the fireplace sat a statue of Mother Mary. Yeah, you read that right, Mother Mary stared at me from the fireplace, and her eyes most definitely followed my every move. She scared the shit out of me, but then, just as quickly as the goosebumps raised on my neck, I felt guilty because, well, Mother Mary. I didn't frequent that room.

There was a butler's pantry between the kitchen and the dining room. It was so cool, with built-in cabinets. There was a drawer that still held my grandfather's things, like a screwdriver and a little hammer. This was also where she hid the cookies for us. Grandma Tripodi always made us her special chicken soup with orzo and always had a cookie jar full just waiting for us. You could expect three or four different kinds of cookies, though they all tasted the same because she kept them marinating in the jar between visits. We didn't care.

Grandma also showered us with freshly laundered and ironed dollar bills. No joke. To this day, I don't know how she cleaned them but she actually washed the bills. She was always very concerned that we not touch dirty money. Ironically, she chain-smoked in her tiny apartment until the air was so thick, we couldn't see the TV. My brother and I would climb on the back of the couch just so we could suck little breaths of fresh air from the tiny cracked transom. Grandma was complex.

A devout Catholic on Sundays, Grandma was less than pleased that we didn't attend church, and she would not-so-subtly share the consequences with me. I remember the day she proclaimed to me that I would never be allowed to be married in a church. I was, like, I don't know, ten?

She reminded me that since I never received communion, a church wedding was a no-go. I wasn't sure I really cared, but I was pretty sure I was offended. Why wouldn't God just be happy that I was marrying?

In retrospect, I suspect that she feared for our souls, and these were the ways she was trying to save us.

Along with the stiff singles and the second-hand smoke, Grandma used to give us holy water that she would bottle up for us from her church. I kind of felt like that was cheating, but her intentions were good, so we played with it. She prayed for us when we left.

It was probably a good thing too because, as a kid, I didn't know how to pray. There were times when I wanted to pray, but I felt like I didn't know how. I hadn't had the lessons, you know, the ones they must give you in bible study, and I felt selfish asking God for stuff when I didn't go to church. It didn't feel fair, and after all, the little exposure I had had to God was that he could be pretty scary. I wasn't even sure this was my God anyway.

So, one night, shortly after I had found my invisible energy ball, I decided I was going to pray. I was going to ask God for something, something neutral, something good, and not just good for me. But just as I was beginning to formulate my words, I began to feel fear. I recalled some movie line in a singsong voice say, "Be careful what you wish for, or it might come true!" I freaked. And all at once, I decided I would not pray for fear that I would ask for something wrong and God would trick me by twisting my prayer or wish into some tragic curse. Yet, in the very same instant, I heard within me a woman's voice, not my own, clearly say, "It doesn't work that way. Intention is everything. God knows your heart." Her voice released my fears, and I never again questioned my prayers or my God, though I was still unsure if my God was the same one I'd heard so much about.

It was a while before I heard her voice again—about twenty-six years, I guess.

Living in between is easy when we are kids, before it's been beaten out of us by society. It's like wind and the magic of nature: it just flows, and kids just get it.

If we are lucky, when we grow up, we remember without fear. When I was in junior high, I used to ride horses at a small stable. Marilyn, the owner, was a single mother to a teenage boy whose face I can't recall. I am not even sure I ever saw through the hair that fell across his face as he briskly walked through the stables, always on his way to more important things. Marilyn was a force, but she also carried with her an air of vulnerability. I couldn't make it out then, but as I look back from an adult's perspective, I can feel the wounds and scars of life, loss, and the pangs of fear as she navigated life alone. She was a strong woman, and she wore her thick salt-and-pepper hair short.

Three decades later, and I can still remember every detail. I was sitting at my desk taking a math test when I saw her. In a flash, my desk, the other students, the room all disappeared, and all I could see was a woman wailing in grief with her hands covering her face. Her salt-and-pepper hair fell over her hands, and her body was convulsing. I gasped and shook my head, and I was brought back to the room. I looked up at the clock: 1:11 p.m.

I felt a shiver start at my forehead and roll across the top of my head down my neck. And then it happened again: everything went blank except for her with her hands over her face and the sound of her sobbing. Fear erupted, and I wondered if I were going crazy. Was this how it happened? One day in math class, you just lose your fucking mind? It took a lot of energy to shut out the crying woman and refocus on my test.

That afternoon I headed to the stables. My favorite horse, Smokey, was an American Paint. He was what they call a push-button horse, and he loved me. I'd click my tongue when I entered the stables, and he would lean out of his stall, calling back to me in anticipation of his carrot. This day was different. All of the horses were in the backs of their stalls, and the air was heavy.

As I made my way to Smokey's stall, I heard her crying. My teeth went metal. You know the feeling when your heart rate shoots up and you can taste your metal fillings? It was the exact same sob I had heard earlier that day.

As I came around the corner, there she was. Marilyn had her head in hands, and she was sobbing, I had never seen this woman look anything other than fierce.

When I asked her what was wrong, she told me that one of the mares had reared up and gotten her leg stuck in the hay rack, breaking it. When the vet arrived to check her out, he recommended she be put down. This mare had just had a foal born with a facial deformity, which would have required special feeding throughout its life. She had to make the decision to put them both down. Through my own tears, I asked her what time this happened.

"Just after 1 p.m.," she said.

Some might suggest I saw her crying because of the connection I had with Marilyn, but I disagree. While I do believe that we are all connected, I believe the message came through Smokey. I had such a strong connection with him, and he had a strong connection with the mare. I have always felt that was the energy line that reached me.

Why wouldn't I have the same connection between a human soul and an animal soul? This intricate web of energy that connects us all is the magic of the Universe. I've tried to explain this to friends over the years but could never find the words.

I was high in college when I saw them, the lines that connect our relationships. I have always felt it and seen it in my mind's eye, but then I could actually see it in the air and put words to it. These lines are different from the web that connects us all. They are the varied

47

shades of gray ropes that extend from the embodied soul of one person to another. Sometimes the lines or ropes are thick, and sometimes they are thin. Some are complicated braids made up of other braided strands. Family can often look like this.

Others are loose and fraying. Once I saw one as a knot, the huge kind of knot you'd expect to see on a massive ship. That relationship was stuck and heavy.

Sometimes one of the lines gets snagged as an intersecting line penetrates it and passes through. Sometimes neither are affected by the intersection. Sometimes the lines merge and continue alongside each other, making both lines stronger together for a time, like the connection I had with Jared.

And if you look deeply enough, some lines are dense, and some are extremely light. Over the years, I've been able to discern what each means to me, from the insignificant crossing of paths to the deep, soul-level connections that forever changed my spirit.

We come here to the physical world to experience the contrast, to learn, to heal, and to expand. An integral aspect of learning is done through relationships. I would be so bold as to claim it's through relationships that we do nearly all of our learning. When we interact with others, our energies connect. A brief nicety on a subway may show as a thin straight line that easily glides through you, perhaps from a less heart-centered position like the leg. A passionate and deeply intense relationship may appear as a thick line from the heart space. If that same relationship is ended and parts of you are emotionally torn away with it, that heart space line may appear snagged and jagged as it passes through your center.

We each have our own translation of this energy language. We all have our own perspective, and it's up to each of us to learn our own dialect. No matter whether you learn the language or not, we all learn from every relationship, even those that end in pain. Throughout our lives, we leave bits of ourselves along the way. But it's your soul's right to be whole, and it's within your power to call yourself back to center.

After my son, Max, died, I was sitting alone in the hospital room barely able to draw enough oxygen to stop the lightheadedness that came with our new reality. My husband, Jared, had gone to walk him to the morgue. He couldn't bear to hand his small, bundled body over to the man who came to take him. He just seemed larger than life, this man. We heard his footsteps and felt them shake the floor as he approached my room. Easily 6' 4" and void of the resonance of compassion, to this day, I can't decide if the expression he wore was of total indifference or skillfully masked empathy. Sitting on that bed, a wave of understanding rolled over me, almost shifting my weight backward.

I understood what people meant when they said it was like having a hole in their heart. My heart felt like Swiss fucking cheese.

Months after we returned home and had slipped back into some of our old routines, I was still Swiss cheese. I mean, I expected to be. In fact, I knew very well our lives would never be the same, our "normal" would never be the same. Some in my inner circle, however, felt that the holes had had enough time to close. This is why they say when you suffer a devastating loss, you often find that you lose your address book too. You discover the depths of the ropes.

Over that first year, while I was shocked at the lack of density to some of my relationships, I was also often surprised that other ropes, previously unnoticed, found their way into deep, soulful braids straight to my heart. One of the gifts of death is seeing with clarity what and who are truly important.

I had begun to try to reconnect with other living people outside of my home. I spent a few hours each week crying on the Pilates machine at my good friend's studio. I walked to the coffee house, numb and still unable to taste the cappuccino no matter how strong I ordered it. I knew I needed a push. I could feel my vibration dulling. My energy was obviously low, but to me, it felt like my frequency continued on a downward trajectory.

I had heard of a soul retrieval somewhere along my grief journey, and I was ready to pull my pieces in, to call my power back to me, but I knew I needed the help of an expert guide. That's when I met Karen. I can't recall how I got her name, but I knew I liked her the first time I stepped through the cloud of sage and mugwort. Nestled in a wooded area in Oregon, her healing space was thick with smoke, decorated with skin drums, feathers, and herbs. I could feel the energy. It was palpable and even though I was nervous walking in, I knew in my heart that I was about to find something that I had been searching for since Max died.

Having your heart ripped from your chest leaves you pretty vulnerable and fearful. I didn't have a whole lot of trust for people I didn't know. You know, having that whole inner circle crumble can really screw with your sense of security. So, lying on her floor surrounded by artifacts and the sounds of drum beats and chanting, I found myself simultaneously sinking into a feeling of comfort and being held while my brain was trying to resort to logic to comprehend what I was asking her to do for me.

In that moment, like so many other moments before and after throughout my life, I decided to lean in and trust my feelings, to ratchet down the logical mind and trust that life, energy, our souls, and the invisible fabric between us all vibrate at tangible frequencies.

I felt a whole lot, actually, and then I didn't. And again I had the choice to trust my feelings. She guided me through a soul retrieval ritual, and we called my soul back to me. It was beautiful. There was an owl's wing, drum sounds I could feel echo inside my chest, visions, chanting, singing, colors, and messages from the divine. Two black crows, my spirit animal, perched on a tree out the window for the entire ceremony, only to fly off when I exited her cabin. I loved every minute.

Afterwards, I buried a totem I made with my own hands in my front yard. Years later, when we moved, I was tempted to unbury it and take it with me, but I decided instead that its energy fed the trees around it. Moving it just didn't feel right. I could breathe just a little bit easier.

Someone asked me if I was fixed after that. It was another one of those moments really only understood by a grieving person. I saw myself deliver a single throat punch, dropping her to the ground, yet I felt compassion because I knew she really was just hoping I was healed. The thing is you don't ever get fixed when the break is so big and the scar is so deep. The branch of your tree regrows, but it does so differently from then on. The tree can still be beautiful and yield fruit in the coming seasons, but the branch that was ripped from the trunk? It leaves a scar that pushes new growth sideways.

These are ways I see my worlds. Give yourself permission to view your own Universe in the way that feels right to you. This is a huge ask, I know. We have been trained for thousands of years to accept other people's translation of God and the meaning of life. Have you ever asked your Self, what resonates with you?

How do we rationalize that thousands of years ago someone got the message from God, but today we aren't special enough to tap into the conversation or have a divine experience?

"Religion is belief in someone else's experience. Spirituality is having your own experience."
- Deepak Chopra

Community and common faith are inspiring, and if you're comfortable with the story of your religion, more power to you in your quest for knowledge and understanding. You can maintain that and still be aware of your individual experience in the Universe and your unique connection to the divine. You can buy into what's been taught to you or not—and still trust your Self first. If you don't, then you are choosing to believe someone else's experience or perception over your own firsthand vantage point.

Your belief system can be unique to you; it doesn't need to be validated by the masses to be truth. I want you to remember a time when you first trusted your inner voice. We all used to. If you think back far enough, you'll remember before you were taught to question yourself.

Take time to understand how you view your own Universe versus what's been taught to you. Feel the freedom to value your own perspective more and to trust your views and experiences over the voice of others. You know what's real for you. Reality is subjective. My Universe is different from your Universe.

Be your own guru.

More about My Universe, the Energy That Connects Us, Soul Contracts, and the Veil:

Lola was just over a year old when she told me that she was my great-grandmother. Like, actually her. I mean, it sorta makes sense. I always have felt a strong connection to Mama Lola. My Lola was named after my great-grandmother, Mama Lola, and she had an undeniable connection with my grandfather, Cagui. If you had seen the first time Lola met my grandfather, you'd wonder too.

Simone was six, Matilda was three, and the twins were about a year old when Lola first met Cagui. We were tired after traveling, but we couldn't wait to see him, so we headed over to visit with fingers crossed that there wouldn't be any major meltdowns.

I don't know if it was because they were so close in age or if they were ultra-empaths or just starving for attention, but a meltdown in our home had a domino effect between the children that, if left unaddressed too long, would knock them down one by one. It was like a virus jumping from one child to the next. If we were lucky, we'd catch it in that familiar whine and then relocate our clan in time to avoid a public display of volcanic expression. So quickly did they move from whining, to boneless puddle, to face melting.

With four kids under six years old, we quickly learned that if we were going to maintain any friendships in life, we would need to spare our tribe the reenactment of Raiders of the Lost Ark. We would need to learn to identify the kids' melting point, at minimum, four minutes before the explosion, so that we could exit stage left. There was more than one occasion when my husband would simply raise an eyebrow to me across the room, and mid-conversation I would continue "uh huh, oh yeah" as I shoved blankies, toys, and sippy cups back into the diaper bag, grabbing my coat, and announcing, "Love you. Thank you. Gotta go!" We were peeling down the driveway before the host knew the door closed.

Our family motto had become, "Leave them wanting more." It worked for us, I think. I mean, we still have friends.

So, when we arrived to see Cagui sitting in a chair across the room, I wasn't surprised when Lola's twin, Rocco, lumbered into the room, spotted Cagui from a distance, and then hauled ass in the opposite direction crying. The older girls gave him a quick hug and took off to the kitchen for snacks. But when I entered the room holding Lola, she saw Cagui for the first time, and she scrambled down my body and speed-crawled to him. I had never seen her move so fast. She cleared his shoes, grabbed his brown polyester pant leg, and hoisted herself up into his arms.

It brought my mother and me to tears. She held his face in her little hands, and they touched noses. My grandfather repeated, "My Lola, my Lola," and something lit up in both of them. It really did feel like a little bit of Mama Lola was with my Lola.

If you could squint your eyes and see the edges of the physical body blur into the space that surrounds it and then notice the energy and vibration of the soul radiating from the center of the body out past those edges—much like a visible sound wave emanating outward and upward—and then if you could follow that energy wave up toward the Universe and notice waves are everywhere and from everyone, accepting that all of this energy connects somewhere above the Universe into a collective pool of blue light that hovers above, then you'd see how I understand our soul connections. We are all a part of this same pool of blue light, vibration, and energy. When a soul decides to manifest in the physical, it's as if this vast blue hand directs a finger downward, and from that fingertip, an individual's manifestation occurs: still connected energetically to the larger blue hand but also separate in its own form. When the soul is finished in the physical form, it leaves the body and reconnects above.

I have heard others suggest our soul is a single grain of sand, and the beach is the collective. Each grain is individual, and yet together we create the beach. My understanding is a little different in that while we are unique in our form, the connection between souls (our energy) in that blue pool can be more fluid. Sometimes, that blue pool can mix, and when a soul comes to physical form, it can share some of the same energy of another. This is why the idea of someone having a bit of someone else inside of them makes complete sense to me. Each person is unique, yes, but sometimes part of one has joined the vessel of another.

I have always understood that souls return to physical form, often in the same circles, throughout multiple lifetimes, and in varied relationships to each other. One lifetime, two souls may come in as friends, another as a mother and daughter, and another as two strangers whose interaction shifts a greater dynamic. You get the idea.

If you think about it, I bet you have experienced an inexplicable bond with someone, a time when you just knew you were connected at a deeper level. We are not just here for ourselves. We learn and teach each other through relationships and connections: the good, the bad, the painful, and the joyful. There is beauty in the contrast and opportunities for growth in all of it.

The contracts we make prior to taking form map points in the physical that, when connected, yield paths to the types of learning we hope to gain at a soul level. My contract intersected Jared's and Max's, yet our paths for learning were so different you might have difficulty seeing how they could possibly complement each other, but they did. They still do — intricate webs of connection, like celestial fabric that when viewed from a distance appear to be a blur of stars and lines, but when seen up close reveal trails of light that weave a beautiful story.

It was 2006 when I was pregnant with Max. Simone was two years old, and Max would complete Jared's and my family. I had a smooth pregnancy with nothing more than the occasional heartburn, which was a welcome contrast to Simone's birth. When Simone was handed to me in the delivery room, I instantly knew she was struggling to breathe. The nurses and doctors responded calmly, assuring this first-time mother that she was just fine, but it was the way her back gently arched and her left side lifted just slightly more than her right when she inhaled that made me yell and demand they come look at her right away. That's when they saw it too and rushed her to the next room.

X-rays revealed that Simone had developed a diaphragmatic hernia during the last stage of my pregnancy. Her intestines had breached the diaphragm and were pressing on her lungs. Her right lung had collapsed during birth. Lucky for Simone, her hernia was on her right side, and her liver had plugged the hole like a cork; her heart was fully developed. Laparoscopic surgery and forty-five days in the NICU, and Simone came home for Thanksgiving.

So, my doctor wasn't surprised when we called her for an urgent appointment at thirty-two weeks pregnant with Max. She had held our hands through Simone's pregnancy and had expected to see signs of worry during this one. But what she didn't realize was that since childhood, I have had a deep connection with my guides. You see, sometimes they gifted me with glimpses through the veil.

That morning I had woken up from a dream, and I turned to Jared and said, "There is a weak point at the point of intersection." It was eerie. I was calm.

"What?" Jared asked.

"There is a weak point at the point of intersection." I could only repeat those exact words. I couldn't alter them; I couldn't decipher them. My doctor saw us right away.

After checking me out, she offered to do an ultrasound to ease my worry and concluded that this was nerves, understandable after Simone's rocky start. She was wrong. I knew it and a panic rose like a spiral of fear building. In that moment, I heard within me that familiar woman's voice, not my own, clearly say, "They won't see it. You've done all you can."

Instantly, her voice melted my fear. I was gently numbed into acceptance and filled with love, unsettled but calm. I'd never been in this space before, feeling so sure of something and at the same time resolved that it simply was. I only heard her three times — that time in the OBGYN office at thirty-two weeks pregnant, again during Max's birth, and during that time shortly after we returned home — but the sensation is similar when I hear or feel others.

Mostly, it's the feeling I get first. I think it's the way the energy frequency field hits me. I feel the consistency of the air change and then information comes through either as images, usually very close up as if an enlarged portion of an image is superimposed over the view of my left eye, or as a feeling of knowing or understanding. Sometimes it's audible. Most times, it's a combination. Usually the imagery is more muted and clearly some sort of translation of a frequency to visual, but a few times it's been like seeing something in the physical.

As they wheeled me into the delivery room, I was overcome with the feeling that my grandfather Tripodi was in the room. I smelled him. It was as if he filled every corner of my head, consuming my focus and filling my heart. I was compelled to say it out loud, and until I did, I could focus on nothing else.

"Grandpa Tripodi is here," I told Jared. Strange: I hadn't felt his presence since I was a child. It was odd but also comforting. In retrospect, I see he was coming to help Max transition.

Teachers and Guides come when we need them and when we ask, but I'll get into that more later. Just like that saying about friends, Guides can also show up in our lives for "a reason, a season or a lifetime." I'll add one more option: "lifetimes." There are soul-level guides. I've always understood it this way: when we are born, some guides choose to stay with us for this entire incarnation, some stay at the soul level throughout our string of lives, and others come and go to help with specific lessons or stages in a life. Grandpa was coming to guide Max, but not in the direction I was expecting.

As labor progressed, I questioned why Grandpa was with me, but I didn't get an answer, just a feeling of his lingering presence over my left shoulder, tucked in close by my ear. When the message is for me, I always feel them really close in, almost like an overlay with my physical body, as if my left shoulder is weighted and my ear is muffled. If the message is for someone else, they feel a little farther away and over my left eye, mostly. I guess it's an inner circle thing, you know, boundaries. I've never questioned it; I just know that is the difference between a guide visiting me for me and one visiting for someone else.

A few hours in, the nurse came over to fiddle with the heart rate monitor. Max, she said, had moved and was evading the monitor. She calmly adjusted the band around my belly. It didn't seem unusual, and we continued talking and giggling. I was in the middle of telling Jared to stop farting. I mean come on! These were like sonic booms shaking the room. What the hell had he eaten?

Only the laughter and the looks exchanged between the nurse and Jared told me that maybe I was missing something. Also, Jared didn't protest, which was a red flag. He always denied it, even if it was just the two of us. Oh, my God, was it the nurse? No, she wouldn't. Would she? Oh my God, it was me.

How did I not know this? Thankfully, at this point, nine months pregnant and bursting at the seams, I really could not give a shit. We laughed. I farted more, apparently.

Max continued to move around, and the nurse came back a bit later to readjust. Routine now, we kept chatting. The difference was, this time my attention was drawn to the nurse, and adrenaline shot through my veins. I lost my hearing, and panic set in fast and hard. It was like my voice was on a radio frequency playing at full volume, but it was only broadcasting inside my skull. "Get a C-section! Get a fucking C-section!"

My inner voice was so loud in my head that I could feel my throat scratch. I had never even contemplated a C-section. Even after Simone's birth, changing my birth plan just hadn't occurred to me, and a C-section hadn't even crossed my mind. I found myself muttering frantically, quiet at first then louder, "Give me a C-section. If you need to give me a C-section, just give me a C-section."

The nurse calmly continued to search for Max's heartbeat. "Honey, you don't need a C-section, he just mo—" She found it. The monitor reset, and Jared exhaled.

"If you need to give me a C-section," I continued. Panic still lingered; I knew I had to say it again. I trailed off. That voice I had heard weeks before was there; she was floating on my shoulder. "You'll never convince her. It's OK. Nothing you say will convince her."

And just like that, my shoulders relaxed. Again, I was in this place of knowing and understanding that no words would alter, calm yet not quite settled. It was almost like being anesthetized, when you're counting back from ten and you want to object or make a joke, but there's no use because seven is fading, and it's much too comfortable to just be.

That was the beginning. Soon after I went into full labor. My doctor was on vacation, so they called in the on-call doc. I had never met this guy. He seemed nice enough, but he was in and out checking my stages, and I wanted my other doctor. She knew us, and she understood why we insisted the NICU nurses be present for Max's birth. I mean, after Simone, I wasn't taking chances. Labor progressed, and the NICU nurses stood against the wall, patiently waiting for Max to arrive so they could get on with their shifts.

They handed me Max; he was perfect. Jared was cutting the umbilical cord, and through tears of joy I looked down at his beautiful face. "Hi, Max," I said.

His mouth formed a perfect circle as he began to draw in breath. Except nothing. His eyes locked on mine, and that's the moment my Universe tilted. What I saw here was very different from what the doctor, the nurses, and even Jared saw. To me, Max's face shifted in an instant. His pupils were dark saucers. His skin was gray, and his lips were blue.

I yelled for help. The nurses leaned in and assured me that he was fine. He passed his APGARs, and to everyone else, he looked just as he should.

"He just needs a little stimulation. Rub his arms. He's just fine," the nurse said with a smile.

"He's not breathing!" I screamed.

They lunged forward. Max was whisked away, and within moments, they transferred him to the resuscitation room. The doctor worked madly to get me patched up. Jared ran to be with Max. We couldn't leave our boy alone.

It took the doctor what felt like an eternity to deliver the placenta and finish up. I had no idea what was happening down there. Blood. Lots of blood. He told me to breathe and that if I could stay still, he could finish faster. His tone was caring and firm, but between the lines I understood something wasn't right. It was taking too long.

He looked up at me and said, "The umbilical cord fell off the placenta. We never see this. It's as if there was a weak point at the point of intersection."

I wailed, screaming at the top of my lungs, "No, not again!" I was aware that other birthing mothers in rooms near me might hear me and be frightened, but I didn't care. My baby was dying. Primal screams came from a bottomless pit of agony that originated somewhere in my gut.

I felt her presence again on my left shoulder. She didn't speak then, but I felt her holding me, and this time I could see her. She lingered in the air above my left shoulder, in and out of the fabric of my being. It was hard to tell where I ended and she began sometimes. I never saw her entire body, and I couldn't look directly at her. She floated there in white swirls of light. Her profile was feminine, and the swirls continued to move around her almost like long hair blending into her dress. She was in constant motion, yet she stayed in the same place.

Over the next two hours, she walked me through Max's life and his death. As the doctors and nurses worked diligently to save Max's life, rushing diagnostic tests and trying procedures, she lifted the corners of the veil for me and confirmed my biggest fears. I knew deep in my heart he was going to die. And each time that knowing rolled over me, I felt like I betrayed him. No! I won't think that, I won't give up, he has to be OK! Oh God, let him be OK, I thought.

Those were the moments she let me process the pieces, patiently lingering as if she were giving me time to sit with the inevitable.

"Take me instead," the words made so much sense to me, a trade. Only, the moment the thought presented itself, I felt time freeze. This was one of those moments when time and space cease to exist as we know them. Instead multiple streams of thought and possibility strike in the exact same moment, almost like rays of light joining together to form a column of many colors. Each ray was a different thought or possibility. Simone, she would have no mommy. Jared, would he be OK? My parents. Max, would the weight of my soul slow his transition? I felt more guilt. How could I even hesitate? Of course, trade me!

She took away all my guilt, thoughts, and questions.

"It doesn't work that way," is all she said, and I knew it didn't.

We all have our own connection to the Universe. While we cling to each other here on earth, we still have our own paths to walk. This sort of download of understanding was comforting and sad and calming and confusing all at once. No, not confusing, that's the thing. Deep inside, it made sense. The times I was confused were the moments I didn't want to consciously accept. Her downloads were just that—the essence of acceptance and love, a beautiful cut from a double-edged sword. Jared and I clung to each other, while the doctors and nurses tried everything. I saw the sorrow in their eyes and the caring in their hearts. Every single one of them felt our pain.

She never left my left side. Jared never left my right side.

Our doctor stayed with us the entire time. He translated the jargon from the NICU staff and patiently repeated things. We were in slow motion, and everything around us was moving so fast.

Choosing the moment your child dies is an impossible decision for a parent. It changes you, even when you know the transition of death is the only gift you can give your child. They had set us up in the room across from the resuscitation room. I was still wheelchair bound and feeling the full effects of the epidural. We spent most of the time with our hands on Max, kissing his forehead as he lay on the table, nurses and doctors in a flurry around him. They moved us back to the room across the hall to explain they'd done all they could and that the only reason his heart was still beating was because of the machines.

The exhausted nurse stood in the doorway. "Don't take your hands off of him! I want to be there the exact moment," I said.

The nurse scrambled back to alert the staff, but something in me feared they already stopped. I stood up and lunged across the room. The doctor yelled to Jared to grab me. I had no feeling in my legs, and I risked breaking something when I couldn't take the next step. I was frantic. I had to get across the hall. Jared swept me into the wheelchair.

I heard her voice. "It's OK. He waited," and my blood pressure dropped. When I entered his room, I saw an orb of light in the upper left corner of the room—yes, just like you see in the movies. The instant we were both through the door, a smaller light left Max's body and met the larger light in the corner. There was no doubt in my heart that it was Grandpa Tripodi and Max.

I am forever grateful that she and my grandpa came to be with us that day. Her guidance allowed me to be present enough to appreciate the small moments I had with Max, to register the softness of his skin, the curls in his thick, black hair, his perfect face looking just like Simone.

She guided me through every moment of his all-too-short life, gently but firmly helping me to navigate my denial and anger and fear. She lifted the veil between the physical and nonphysical and allowed me to drift between the two. She reminded me to listen to the soul not through my ears, but through my heart and to lean into that beautiful fabric that connects us all. While I never saw her again, she stayed with me for months after Max died. Peeling back the corners and sharing bits of truths helped me to hold onto a Universe that had been forever tilted off its axis.

Max's soul contract didn't extend long past birth, yet the depth and impact of his brief visit shifted my soul. I often wondered why he would agree to staying for such a short time. Was it more a lesson for us? Why would I ever agree to be a part of this? I doubt I'll ever understand it all. I don't expect we're supposed to. I have seen some of the gifts he brought to us, and his death taught me everything I know about life. An unexpected teacher, he taught me the truth about life, the truth about Max.

> *The truth about Max*
> *is that life is fluid, like an energy ball racing*
> *toward physical bodies*
> *staying for a time only to dislodge from the*
> *confines of skin and bone*
> *to move forward toward its next transition.*
>
> *The truth about Max is we are here to*
> *experience . . . everything.*
>
> *Love. Despair. Joy.*
>
> *The truth about Max is that we are not alone,*
> *and we travel this life with others.*
> *Some are present in the physical world*
> *and others are connected by the energy which*
> *makes up our soul matter.*

The truth about Max is that he shared secrets with me. He reminded me that living is greater than the bodies we visit in.

The truth about Max is that his short life opened my eyes to what living actually means, he helped dispel the myth of life and death, and he taught me to trust — above all else — my intuition, my internal compass, yes, those voices in my head.

All of these experiences and the ones I will have in the future define and will redefine how I understand my Universe, the ever-expanding evolution of my spirituality. I am comfortable with the unknown parts, and I am confident it will reveal itself when I'm ready.

It's no secret: You know deep inside that you can trust your own experiences and feelings about your Universe.

Exercises & Reflections:

Finding your Universe is looking within your Self, validating your experiences and ideas and trusting that your perception has an important place in defining the Universe as you know it. Whatever your belief system is, if it feels right to you, go with that. And if something feels off, maybe give yourself the freedom to consider that you may have some inside information. After all, we are all divinely connected.

This is the time to give yourself permission to explore like you used to as a child, led by experiences and joy. This isn't about ghost stories or darkness. There is nothing fearful about connecting with your loved ones and guides. When you only focus on the love, love is what you get.

Perhaps some of my stories resonated with you or triggered some memories. Maybe you feel secure in your current view of the Universe. Reflecting on your Universe comes more easily when you're in the right frame of mind. So find a quiet comfortable spot free from interruptions and do a 5- to 10-minute mediation to get you focused. You can use a meditation app or simply set a timer and focus on breathing for 10 minutes. Clear your mind, let go of the day, release what's coming next, allow the to-do and grocery lists to fade away and just relax. When you get to this place of feeling calm, your heart rate slows and your soul opens up. This is the place where you'll more easily be able to recall specific experiences or times in your life and even old held theories.

Grab your favorite pen and your workbook or journal.

1) *What is true to you?* This isn't a right or wrong answer and this is not a test of your faith. I just want you to be ok with the possibility of more. Love what you believe and be open to more.

   Think of a time(or times) in your life when what you experienced didn't match what the physical world has defined as true. A connection with a loved one who has passed. A knowing or download. A hunch. A dream.

   How did you feel, emotionally and physically? Did you doubt it? Why? What was the thought just before the doubt?

2) *Validate your stories.* Bring yourself back into that moment when you knew it was true or happening. How did you feel? What was your experience, regardless of what makes "sense." Let go of the ego and the need to rationalize and write about the sensations and emotions and connection you felt. This sort of self-validation is freeing and is something you can recall to remind yourself of your experience. For years, when I first began my

energetic practice, I would keep a specific journal about my experiences because it was all too easy to rationalize away what was so real in the moment. On the days I doubted myself, I only needed to review my journal to be filled with confidence again.

Share your stories with someone who understands. You might be surprised to find they also have had similar experiences. Don't have anyone in your tribe? Join the conversation at JeanineTripodi.com/WSGS.

3) *Listen to the Universe.* Meditate. Getting quiet in your mind is the best way to hear your connection.

4) *Meditation doesn't need to take hours.* Carve out 10 minutes a day. The more consistent you are the faster you'll connect. This takes time. Don't give up. If you are new to meditation you may find that your mind wanders or races. This is normal. Just breath and trust that whatever you are getting out of the time is exactly what you need in that moment. Be gentle with yourself. Meditation is that moment when you have closed the doors to the past and closed the doors to the future and you are just in this one moment. It's ok to bounce back and forth.

Here are some meditation tips: let go of any expectations. Set a timer so you don't have to watch the clock. You can also use an app like Insight Timer that offers background music while you meditate. Sit comfortably and don't worry about getting into a pose or sitting on the floor. Breathe. It's often helpful to focus, for example, on the sound of the music and how it flows through the air and connects with your body. Focus intently on the sound and vibration of the music until you are in an observational state. Any thoughts that pop into your mind can be acknowledged and released as if the thoughts are balloons floating away into the distance. The more you practice this the more easily you will access your higher Self. You can enter meditation with an intention or question and then observe what comes up in a peacefully detached way.

Jeanine Tripodi

Chapter 3

Jeanine Tripodi

Secret #3:
Tap into the Voice of Your Soul

So, you've taken time to reflect on the Universe that is yours to understand. You have put in the time to go through the worksheets and dive deeply into your own personal views, regardless of how they may seem to others. Maybe you've read my story and decided than my views are bullshit. That's cool. We all have unique experiences, definitions, and truths. It's about finding your own perspective. I want you to hear the voice of your soul and to listen.

Individual perspectives vary, but there are common techniques everyone can use to access their soul's voice. They all start with heart. Let's begin by recognizing the heart as the landing point of your soul.

In *The Seat of the Soul*, Gary Zukav explains that, "In the creation of the personality the soul calibrates parts of itself, reduces parts of itself, to take on the human experience" (page 71). In other words, in this current human form, you are merely the physical expression or extension of part of your soul. On a soul level, you are still connected to its entirety.

Intelligence is held both in the heart and the brain, but heart intelligence holds more truth. Thoughts are run through the filter of the ego. Heart-based direction comes straight from your soul. Work them together, and the golden path twinkles before you. Tap into heart intelligence for answers.

This is what I call your heart's truth. This is your intuition and connection not just to your higher Self, but to the divine support system and divine matrix that connects us all to each other and to that which is greater than ourselves. Tap in here, and you are communing with the cosmos.

Leading with your heart's truth allows you to more closely follow the path of your soul. But don't lose sight of the gifts of the brain, the ability to choose the how and when of our actions. The mistake many make is to bypass the heart's truth altogether, ignoring intuition and emotions and following only the brain. This is choosing to be led by the ego. But don't forget, the filter of the ego is painted by culture, family, religion, past experiences, environment, and fabricated rules and expectations from the outside. Then there are some who choose to follow only their heart, ignoring the possibility that our heart's truth may benefit from being rolled out in more conscious steps. Intuition can be contaminated by fear, and that's when you must apply your intellect.

While I encourage us all to first tap into heart intelligence, balancing inner wisdom with common sense feeds the clarity of next steps in a human world and is the fastest way to shine the light on your path. This is the definition of heart-centered living.

Let your heart lead.

Be guided by your own purpose.

Intuition cannot be explained by the five senses. It shows up as emotions and as feelings in the body. It nudges like an inner knowing. An inexplicable clarity. It must be felt. It's something you learn to trust without having to explain, and while answers will always come, they may not be the ones you expect or prefer.

The soul's voice doesn't bargain or rationalize. It is nonjudgmental, and it speaks only for you. You cannot call on it for answers or guidance *for* another person, they must use their own intuition — though it will help you to discern another person. True intention is read through energy and oftentimes shows up as a gut feeling. Emotions are the messages of the soul.

Ask and listen. You may hear the answer in your own inner voice, you may simply know what the answer is, or you may feel it in your body. If you're new to listening to your intuition, be open to any and all combinations of receiving the information you seek.

Your soul's voice is quick, concise, and direct. Answers often come before you even finish asking the questions. If you're honest with yourself, the intuitive information feels right, whether you like the answer or not. Negotiating with your inner wisdom is futile and questioning it yields the same response, unless you've let your ego take over.

Your higher Self and, by extension, your guides will help you to see the illuminated paths to expansion, but they will not make the decision of which to take. Free will and all. You will be supported in whichever path you choose, and if you're open to the larger lesson, you will learn from all of them. Sometimes we choose to learn through joy, and other times we choose to learn through pain. Your soul is more concerned with the bigger picture of growth. How you get there is up to you; there are many paths to the same destination.

Allowing yourself to feel through your world is the epicenter of heart-centered living. Using a heart-centered approach to guide your life always leads you back to your soul.

My mother used to tell me, even as a young girl, "Follow your heart." I think she knew from when I was a young child that I navigated the world a little differently.

Being an all-in sort of gal, I took this saying to heart. I chose the full-on feelings route of life. I suffer no fools (though my definition of a fool is one who is inauthentic, not unintelligent). I live with big ups, big downs, and the conscious choice to regret as little as possible, to see the lessons in the dirt on my face, and to lean toward hope and joy, even if I can't see the next step on the path.

Unless, of course, I am feeling paralyzing fear, because you know that happens too, and anyone who pretends they have gotten where they have without that is probably full of shit. In other words, I have made some serious mistakes, and I still wouldn't change a thing. Well, that's not entirely true. I would change a few things, but I can't, and it has all led to this place in time and space. So, let's move forward.

To this day, I believe if the things we do aren't coming from a place that feels good, we should reconsider the motive. Why do we run toward things that feel less than joyful? It's time to get real honest with yourself about what drives you. The resulting emotions of any actions launched from a place of fear or guilt are incapable of yielding the good feelings you seek.

That isn't to say every move I make generates happiness, but my goal every day is to move toward what feels good and away from what feels bad. It's pretty simple, really. I lead this way, knowing full well that there is beauty in the contrast and lessons in the pain. It isn't the absence of challenges that drives me, but rather the hope and expectation of joy. When we are feeling joy or whatever it is we want to feel, we exude those frequencies. We literally vibrate at the frequency of our emotions, and what we send out, we draw back into ourselves. So through it all, the anger, tears, gratitude, and laughter, we are calling to ourselves the frequency we send out.

You are responsible for the frequency you broadcast.
Let that one sink in a minute.

While we can't control everything we'd like to in this world, we can manage our response to people and circumstances, and, as a result, calibrate our vibration and what shows up in our lives moving forward. The emotions you feel as you bump up against people and things in your life are directional signs straight from your soul. Be open to the possibility that it isn't always about moving away from discomfort; sometimes the lesson is leaning into the friction. Following your heart's truth isn't about avoidance; it's about trusting your intuition and accessing your connection with the Universe.

If you're going to tell me that you don't have intuition, you can leave that excuse at the door. Intuition is a naturally born gift; everyone has it. Some just haven't unwrapped it yet. If you don't feel like you have intuition, you're either not listening, or you don't like the answers you're getting.

Intuition doesn't placate; it's your direct connection to your inner truths. This inner wisdom may challenge what you prefer, and your ego or human self will try to rationalize what it wants. Overriding your soul with your brain is a human response to discomfort. So are self-doubt and fear.

Intuition uses your physical body as a tell. Pay attention to that inner voice, and you'll start to notice patterns. You can learn to decipher your own code and discern between fear, ego, and intuition. We're going to talk more about how to learn to recognize intuition in the worksheet section.

On several occasions, I have shocked myself at the intensity of my automatic physical response to this inner wisdom. Those times were so unexpected and intense that I didn't need to waste time trying to rationalize my response. I followed my gut without question.

November 3rd, 2007, I went into early labor with my second daughter. It was the one-year anniversary of Max's birth. I couldn't imagine them sharing a birthday; they needed their own celebrations of life. So I did what any partially delusional, grief-slogging mother would do: I ignored labor pains and delivered Matilda the next day.

Exactly one year prior, I desperately wanted to stop my breasts from lactating. Producing milk after Max died was yet another betrayal of my body. Yet when Matilda arrived, I struggled to make enough to keep her tiny five-pound frame fed. I ate everything on the list. I drank a beer. I got rest. It was still not enough. So when my doctor prescribed a medication that could help increase my milk production, I had it filled immediately.

When I picked up the medication from the pharmacy something felt off. They handed me the prescription vial, and I had a quivery feeling in my throat. My hand started to shake. I returned to my car and sat for a moment, wondering what this meant. Did I even want to nurse? How could I not want to?

Guilt set in. That bitch creeps in whenever there is a crack in a mother's armor. I should want to do everything I possibly can to nurse my baby. What would the other mothers think?

I called my friend Carol. She had also experienced the loss of her baby; she'd understand what was going on in my head. Maybe this was PTSD. Maybe I wanted to nurse but just couldn't because of Max.

Carol listened. She understood the importance of hearing my feelings and trusting them over what the head said. I told her my fears. I analyzed. I rationalized. I decided to take them.

The second I resolved to take the prescription, the vial burned in my hand. I involuntarily and violently threw it onto the floor of the passenger side and gasped. There was no question and no reason; I could not take the pills.

Adrenaline surged through my body, and I began to cry. It was like my head was filled with loud static. I couldn't make sense of it, but I knew without question my inner wisdom had had enough and had simply taken over. I went home and told my husband, who was supportive of my inexplicable logic, as always. I fed Matilda as much as I could and gave her bottles of formula as needed. Since I was bottle feeding, as well as nursing, my husband had the opportunity to snuggle with her on the couch or rock her to sleep while feeding her. She gained weight, and all was well. About a year later, while driving through town, I caught a report on the radio about the potential link between medications that increased lactation and life-threatening conditions.

You do not need to justify the knowing that comes from within. When you trust the messages you get and feel the connection with your soul's voice, you no longer need to convince anyone else of its existence. You do you. It's a beautiful way to live.

Everyone has access to their intuition, but if you're feeling like your inner voice is a distant whisper, there are ways to turn up the volume.

Learning to tap into your intuition—that inner compass—and letting it guide you creates a life that unfolds before you, driven by your soul in alignment with your core truths.

When you ignore this inner guidance, you are creating a life that requires more force and work and friction. You can still sail from A to B, but tapping in and using your compass makes navigating those waters much more smooth and joyful.

First, give yourself permission to listen to that positive and hopeful voice inside your head, that knowing that floods you. That inner nagging warning system is the one our culture tells us to ignore. Your voice and your divine support system are unique to you. Those signs, that synchronicity, that coincidence, that seemingly random connection, thought or observation: these are your team rooting for you, nudging you, and guiding you. That's your higher Self, your inner voice, and your intuition.

Your subconscious mind is your energetic body is your soul is your intuition.

Steve Jobs said,

> *"Intuition is more powerful than intellect."*

He was right. We have access to this wellspring of support and knowledge. Tap in.

We have all heard of women's intuition. Well, men have it too, but as women, we are connected to nature and the moon and the ocean tides and the divine in ways that make us special. Embrace that. As fierce, divine beings it is our responsibility to step into our hearts and to live in alignment with those truths.

Intuition

is clouded

when the

base emotion

is fear or anger.

So, bringing yourself into a grounded and centered place gets you out of the ego (fear, anger) and into your heart. Driving choices from this place is the difference between making a split-second decision or reaction that comes from the wellspring of knowledge within and the choice that is generated from outside pressures or assumed expectations of fear and anger.

So, how do you turn it on? How do you ACTIVATE it?

You don't. The station is already playing; you just need to listen. I'm going to teach you how to turn up the volume. You've already opened yourself up to the connection by giving yourself permission to listen. Now turn up the volume with these three steps.

1. Tune in and Trust

2. Acknowledge

3. Practice

Tune into yourself and trust what you get

Our physical bodies deliver signs all the time, listen: acute feelings of dread, goosebumps, chills up one side of the body, a clear KNOWING, an inner voice, shakes, an expansion of the chest, a physical leaning in. These are some of the ways your higher Self may communicate with your physical being. Take notice, become aware of your own patterns, and most importantly, trust what you get.

Years ago, I was driving home on a neighborhood road I had taken hundreds of times. It was dark, and there were few streetlights on this gently winding road. My water bottle fell on the passenger-side floorboard, and I contemplated grabbing it. I paused but then decided to quickly reach down. The instant my eyes left the road I heard this inner voice very loudly demand, "Look up!"

Without hesitation, I sat upright, and to my horror, I saw a man dressed in all black riding his bicycle on the side of the road. He was swerving slightly and had been absolutely invisible just a moment before. If I had questioned that voice for even one millisecond, that night would likely have ended tragically. The biker continued on quite unaware of what could have been. I was shaken but so appreciative that my guides were present, grateful that I listened without question, and thankful that I learned this lesson without harming anyone.

Paying attention to the ways in which your soul's voice communicates with you is the way to decipher your own secret code. I had learned years ago that when this inner voice speaks, I can trust it as truth. I have also learned that when I am speaking with someone and I have chills down the right side of my body, the message I am delivering is resonating with spirit. When I have bilateral chills, the message I am delivering is resonating with spirit and connecting in the physical to resonate with the person with whom I am speaking.

As you continue to tune into your own code and trust what you get, you will decipher your own patterns and codes that will help you to understand your intuition more clearly. You may not be able to explain this code to others, and I am here to tell you that you don't have to. Someone else's understanding of your intuitive perspective is not vital to your truths.

In all of this work, there is an important piece here: trust. Trust really comes down to choosing. Do you choose to believe yourself and your personal experiences, or do you choose to stay in the shared perspective that requires others to validate your understanding?

Acknowledge

As you start to tune in, be sure to acknowledge the messages you receive from your intuition and from your guides and teachers. Actively appreciating the communication you get from your higher Self reinforces the vibrational signal that you are open and interested in receiving more information.

Acknowledge. Say thank you. Pray. Smile at the stars. Send that loving appreciation back.

If you are doubting whether you are communing with your intuition or your conscious mind, I get it. It's normal. Sometimes we need proof. So, do yourself a solid and start a journal. Journal all of the times that you can remember when you felt like you had some sort of inner knowing. Describe the situation or person. Write down how you felt in detail. What information did you get and how? Where did it show up in your body? In your heart? Your gut? Your chest? What did it feel like? A nagging? A heavy weight? A knowing?

Looking back, was your gut feeling accurate? Start to map the information received to the way it shows up to the accuracy of the information. I still do this because sometimes our codes expand and we have more to work with, and sometimes fear is tricky, and it's a vicious survivor. It's good to have reminders that you can trust your Self.

We will get into this in detail in the workbook section. This is where you learn to decipher your own code.

Knowing how fear and intuition show up differently in your physical body makes it easier to discern between the ego and the soul's voice. My dad was a worst-case-scenario sort of prepper. Not like a doomsday prepper, more like, "Hey, I grew up in Boston in the fifties, and I have raised you in a bubble in the suburbs, so let's teach you some serious street smarts by running worst-case scenarios like a game."

He taught me to think quickly and not panic; those are pretty badass skills. I also ran for many years with the belief that holding onto some fear kept you safe. I'm not a huge fan of that logic anymore.

We'd be driving down the streets of Boston and he would look down the dark side alley. He'd ask, "Jeanine, what if you were walking home at night and it was raining. You had to get out of the pouring rain, but your apartment was blocks away. You could cut through there to shave off some time. What do you do?" That was an easy one.

"Jeanine, that guy there, the strong one, what if he grabbed your arm? What's your move?"

You get it.

When I was twenty, we had some good family friends who were retired FBI agents. The horror stories/tips I took back to school! I knew exactly what to do if someone ever pulled a gun on me and demanded I get in the car. Run, by the way; you run if that happens. Also, don't hang on to that visual because the chances of that happening are slim, and I don't advise playing that scenario more than once. All you need to know is just fucking run.

So, by the time I got to college, I had zero problems speaking up about, well, anything, I guess. I knew a lot of women who would err on the side of self-doubt, hesitating to say something about a situation or person that made them feel off, not wanting to look hysterical or make a guy feel bad.

I was more comfortable responding to my gut and took the risk of being called a bitch—which, incidentally, I was called by a few stellar guys, like the asshole who snuck past my roommate and crept into my bedroom at 1 a.m. to sit at the foot of my bed and watch me sleep. As much as I loved my girlfriends, I felt like they actually minimized my fear and experience. Maybe they never played the worst-case scenario game. This asshole watched me sleep. Who knew what could have come next?

My father trained me to bypass polite mode, and it saved me more than once. That said, oftentimes I would run scenarios that didn't need to be processed, and there was a time in my life when I conjured more fear than I needed. It took me a while to figure out that fear was not a good motivator for me, not in life and not in business. That's when I realized that there was a difference between fear and intuition, and I began to focus on learning to discern between the two.

So, outside of a scenario where you may be in immediate physical danger, because that has different rules, how do you discern between fear and intuition? You get grounded, fast.

Take a deep breath and put your hand on your heart. As you breathe in for the count of five, visualize a white light from above pouring through your core, spreading up, out, and down, connecting you instantly to the divine above and the earth below. It doesn't need to make sense. You are feeling this, not thinking it. Repeat this simple visual until you can feel the light fill your body and radiate up, out, and down as you continue to breathe in for five and out for five.

This type of grounding exercise pulls you out of a parasympathetic state and tells your system to relax. It brings you into the moment and into your body. We want to drive decisions from this place of balance and alignment.

How are you feeling? Scan your body. Are you launching from a space of balance? No? Repeat #1. Don't rush this moment. This is it; this is where you tap in, find balance, and hear your secret code. This is where you begin to see where and how your intuition sends signals to your physical body. Map them through journaling, and you'll begin to see patterns to help you discriminate between fear and intuition. (More on this in the Exercises & Reflections section.) Say thank you. Feel gratitude. Acknowledge that you are experiencing the signs.

Practice

Yeah, there's homework here: practice. The more you tune in, trust, and acknowledge, the more quickly you will learn the secret code to your intuition, and the more quickly you'll recognize the voice of your soul.

Do this visualization every day. Meditate every day, even for just five minutes. You are training yourself to tune in differently. It becomes a pattern. Like a muscle, you have to work it.

It's no secret: Intuition is a naturally born gift. Everyone has it; some just haven't unwrapped it yet.

Exercises & Reflections:

Most people can recall a time when they had a strong gut feeling about another person or situation. Get comfortable, take some deep breaths, and get ready to tap in. But before you start writing, get back into that beautiful meditative state you accessed in the last chapter. Recalling memories and the emotions tied to them is easier when you have accessed a place of calm and connection. Great, now break out your workbook or journal.

1) *Think of a time when you felt inexplicably unsafe.* Where did it show up in your body? Was it a pit in your stomach—chills along your neck? Recall every sensation and emotion that flooded you.

2) *Think of a time when you had a gut feeling and it turned out you were right.* Bring yourself back to that moment and recall how you felt. Where in your body did you feel this intuition? How did it show up?

3) *Think of a time when you had a gut feeling and it turned out you were wrong.* Bring yourself back to that moment and recall how you felt. Where in your body did you feel this intuition? How did it show up?

4) *Learn to discern between fear and intuition.* Repeat steps 2 & 3 as many times as you can. This is mapping your physical tells to accurate or inaccurate gut feelings. Fear and intuition show up differently in the body. Mapping is how you will decipher your own code so that, in the future, you will be able to determine more easily if that nagging gut feeling is intuition or fear.

Jeanine Tripodi

Chapter 4

Jeanine Tripodi

Secret #4:
Tell Better Stories

When I was two years old, we were visiting my grandparents in Puerto Rico. My brother was giving me a piggyback ride, and I lurched backward out of his grip. I landed on the glass coffee table and split open my skull. I remember scenes from this accident, like my mother crying as she held both sides of my head with a bloody dish towel, the dashboard of the car as my father sped through town, and the doctor putting a piece of paper on my butt with a little hole in it where he would give me a shot in my cheek. I distinctly remember being really pissed off that they took my undies and being super humiliated to get a shot in my ass in front of strangers. I don't remember much else. Other than that, I cannot recall going to an emergency room ever in my life. Unless you cracked your skull or broke your bones, it just wasn't done.

Since 2006, the year Max was born, we have frequented the ER more times than I want to admit. I'm pretty confident that new car the doc was driving was courtesy of our family. Rocco was our frequent flyer, not because he is clumsier than his sisters, but because, without even realizing it, our stories changed after Max died.

Life is fragile.

Children die.

It's true. Children do die and life is fragile, but that was not the story we needed to retell ourselves in sheer panic every time Rocco's fever pushed 103 or when he complained of a mystery pain.

We started to call ourselves the 3 percent family. It was reference to the fact that we have been told on many occasions that the chances of our experiencing the medical anomaly at hand was around 3 percent. The random allergic reaction, the combination of the number and types of his birthmarks, the diaphragmatic hernia on her right side, and the umbilical cord tearing from the placenta were all remote chances. So whenever a doctor said to us, "There's a very small chance," we were like, "Yeah, that means nothing to us." We were primed for fear; it was our story.

Many of our ER visits were necessary, but one specifically—make that two—could have been entirely avoided if my son had not been such a phenomenal thespian. He's a skilled method actor, really. Now, I am not saying he faked this at all, I'm suggesting he picked up the story we were telling ourselves and adopted it because the stories we tell and believe can be picked up and accepted by those around us.

One day he was feverish on the couch. My husband went to palpate his abdomen because that's the first thing any parent who has had lighting strike twice does when there is a fever. You know, assess for the remote possibility of acute appendicitis. Rocco knew the drill and what we were checking for.

The moment Jared's hand pressed and released the lower right abdomen, Rocco levitated off the couch screaming. We caught it before it burst! Jared threw me my coat, and I hauled ass to the hospital. Within ninety minutes, we were checked in, checked out, and Roc had enjoyed his $500 Popsicle as we walked back to the car. They sent us home with orders to see our primary care in the morning. The next day, our primary care performed similar tests with similar results.

"Head back to the ER. I think he may have appendicitis. You don't want it to burst."

Well, no shit.

Back in car, parked at ER, checked in, X-rayed, checked out, $500 Popsicle. No appendicitis, and miraculously his fever broke within an hour of returning home. What are you gonna do? As parents, we can get stuck in old stories, but you can forget about trying to change them when your kid is sick and the doctors are inadvertently supporting your fears. A grand in popsicles aside, I am glad we chose to get him checked out. But I do wonder, if we had had a different story about little boys and hospitals, would we have triggered this chain of events and reactions?

We do our best now to look through a different lens when it comes to determining emergencies, though I'm sure, if there is too much gray area we will always err on the side of caution.

The stories you tell yourself and believe shape your life, the choices you make, and the opportunities you see in front of you.

So, when did these stories begin? Some stories are picked up at an early age from those around us, others are developed through our experiences and observations, and some we bring into our lives at birth. Some of these belief systems are deeply ingrained paradigms and opinions that we simply accept as part of our identity. They're often left unexamined. Sometimes these beliefs are inherited from our families or circles of friends.

It's time to observe these as patterns so that you can begin to break those that don't serve you.

The stories that inspire and foster confidence and compassion are growth-building beliefs, such as knowing that there are more good people in the world than bad, the concept that leading with love brings you back to your soul, and the confidence that you will achieve that goal and things will work out. These are the stories created through soul-centered navigation. Write more of these.

Focusing on old, outdated belief systems keeps you anchored in the past. Tell better stories, and you empower yourself to create a new map for your future. You begin to broadcast a frequency that connects with the wholeness of the Universe, physical, and nonphysical. The best mindset is fed by your soul. As you begin to tell yourself better stories, cull them from your Self.

We live in a culture that teaches a story of separation and fear. The media highlights the most horrible stories to sell papers. Reality TV paints a faux picture of life enhanced by manufactured drama. Neighborhoods are divided by politics, religion, and race. Young girls are told in every fairy tale, advertisement, and beauty magazine that they are not strong or beautiful enough. Don't buy into it.

Live through your own perspective. Outstretch your arms—yeah, right now. Stretch them out. Go with me here: everything inside of your fingertips is your theater and your aura/main energetic system. Everything outside of your fingertips is other people's theater. As you walk this lifetime, you bump into other people's energy, and your theaters overlap. Staying within your own aura and operating from this view is living in your true perspective. Stay in this vantage point, and you live your truths guided by your intuition and higher Self.

If you choose to operate and create in your world at the edge of your aura, you are receiving everything that's out there, and everything out there begins to dictate your thoughts and feelings. Shifting your mindset by visualizing better stories must come from a centered place of self, or you end up following other people's paths.

In other words, when you live in this space and not at the edge of your aura, which is so influenced by others' reality, you are grounded and rooted. Then you begin to perceive your world through your own lens, your own perspective.

This doesn't mean you are isolated from other people's realities or the rules of society at large. It simply means you are driving your life from within. You are driving the big and little choices with the intention of living your chosen reality. It becomes the makeup of all of the big and little movements that create your path. You are then living from the inside out.

You are your thoughts, and your thoughts are your truth. Memories of the past or images of the future can either lift you up or take you down. What many people fail to recognize is that they have the power to choose. The intention of your thoughts affects your energy and thus creates your reality.

You are not a static system. Energy is continuously flowing through you, and with each thought and emotion, this energy is being shaped, both consciously and unconsciously. The electrical charges of thought fired by your brain are steeped in intention. It's this intention that shapes your world.

So how do you choose to mold it?

First, you need to understand what your stories are, then you can work to change them. I have had a money story (and not the abundant kind) for years. I have tried to make shifts, repeat mantras, take online courses promising to teach me to bust the beliefs. You name it, I tried it. Here's the thing: it's pretty hard to shift your mindset when you aren't clear on what your mindset is.

In order to shift them, you have to be brave enough to look at your stories and dig deep enough to see how they're rooted. It took years of brutal honesty with myself to begin to decipher how mine had formed. Then came some clarity. I had told myself it was fear of scarcity and instability, but that these were the facts of life for an entrepreneur. When I took a hard look at things, I saw a pattern. For years, whenever my husband and I made great quantities of income, we lost it.

I had a great-paying, soul-sucking job. I left it, and we lived on savings until it was gone. We had wildly successful times during our construction years, and we survived the crash a lot longer than most, until we didn't. The market plummeted, and we lost it all and then some.

Sometimes, my husband and I would have different ideas of how to spend or save; more than once we had a business investment go south. Through these experiences, I built a tragic belief around money: when we make money, it is taken away. Losing money is frightening, unsettling and out of my control. Therefore, earning big money leads to suffering. So, for a while, this belief system prevented us from earning to our potential. For those who are wondering how a belief system can create direct cause and effect like this, don't forget the subconscious and conscious minds work all the time to nudge us forward or hold us back, to create confidence or self-doubt, and to twist the perspective of situations and opportunities. The choices we made and the responses we had to situations were based on our reality, our belief systems.

Some would explain this simply as the Law of Attraction. Like attracts like. When you consciously choose to tell better stories and commit to them, your thoughts change their electrical signals, and your system responds. You broadcast a new signal. This has energetic consequences. While, I agree that the energetic frequency we broadcast draws back to itself that of like frequency, I would also add that there is another piece often overlooked: the subconscious filters we create and through which we view and subsequently respond to our world.

Let's use a cracked car windshield as an example. The Law of Attraction or the energetic consequence of a cracked car windshield may come in the form of feeling frustrated and thus attracting more opportunities to feel frustration. Like attracts like.

The subconscious filter, however, is the way in which you view and perceive the world around you. Like when you have a crack in your windshield, and then suddenly you notice every other car that has a crack in its windshield. This is the result of viewing through the lens of your newly created subconscious filter. In other words, where your attention goes, the energy flows.

Let's look at this in a positive light. Can you recall a time when you felt grateful? Truly grateful? You likely noticed around the same time that there were other areas and relationships in your life for which you also felt grateful. The day just bursts with gratitude because whatever you focus on, you will find. So, when you conjure feelings of gratitude and really allow them to be experienced, you're then tuned into gratitude and it shows up — or becomes more visible — in your life. You become a tuning fork for gratitude.

Manifest Your Life in Three Easy Steps. [Insert eye roll.]

But no, really, you should be manifesting the shit out of your life.

Look, I wholeheartedly believe in the Law of Attraction (LOA) and the methods to manifest, but the word "manifest" has been hijacked even more tragically than the word "organic." If your social media tracking is anything like mine, every other spam email and Facebook post you see in your feed claims to teach you "how to manifest your dream life in three easy steps."

For those of you who may not be clear on how to manifest and what the LOA is, let me break it down in a nutshell.

You think thoughts, you conjure up the feelings these thoughts evoke, and you create an internal reality of already experiencing that which you would like your life. This is the basic approach to manifesting. It works. You also have to practice this state of being even as the reality outside of your eyelids says otherwise. Fake it 'till you make it, but you have to *feel* it and believe it. You see, the thoughts and the feelings together shift that broadcasted signal, and the Universe responds.

The Law of Attraction also works using this signal. Like attracts like. What you put out, via the frequency of your thoughts and emotions, attracts that of similar frequencies. So tune into what you want, center into your own theater, and create from there.

A word on positive affirmations: some people rely on reciting affirmations written by others and then wonder why the flow of manifestation feels more like a damned river. Echoing someone else's affirmation may be a fine place to start, but for it to effect change in your energetic system, you have to *feel* it. You also have to feel it *now*, like it's happening already. So repeating, "I am ready to receive abundance!" is a nice thought that tells the Universe you are waiting. Experience the emotions, commune with your God, the cosmos, and the Universe, and become it. Don't be an observer waiting for it. Own the outcome.

Warning: when mindset becomes delusion, that's when you gotta check yourself. The power of the mind is so strong that you will start to believe what you tell yourself is truth.

This can be a great thing, like when you want to refuse to succumb to that cold, and through mindset, you amp up your immune response. Or when by sheer determination and will, you complete that Portland marathon less than a year after your daughter was born.

I've done both these things, and I can promise you that my finishing those 26.2 miles complete with forty-seven bathroom stops was accomplished by sheer mental imagery. Throughout the race (which, incidentally, my children still think I won), I was all over the map with mindset. I had told myself that the first nine miles would be the hardest, and then I would find my groove. I was in my stride and popping gel shots at mile eleven. Then, just as soon as I felt that inner strength bubbling over, doubt punched me in the jibs and shifted my reality. (Jibs is what my kids call testicles. Don't judge. We also use proper anatomical names. Also, I don't really have testicles.)

As I struggled to outpace the eighty-four-year-old gentleman speed walking ahead of me, I started to listen to that ugly inner voice, you know, that one that tells you, "You suck."

He is literally the oldest man you know.

You're a quitter.

This sucks. You don't have to finish.

I let out a sigh and stumbled as I reached out for the mini KitKat bar the lady on the sidewalk was handing out. I grabbed three, actually.

"You can do it!" she screamed, and I decided to believe her for a moment. I licked the last bits of chocolate off my sweaty palms and shifted into second gear. I brought to mind all the long runs that I had actually enjoyed during training. I told myself that I could do it. Then I doubted it again. Prior to training, I had never run more than five miles. Wait, can I do this? So I decided to focus on enjoying it instead. This I could hold on to. The high I felt after twelve-mile training runs. The accomplishment I felt after going farther than I had ever gone before. So I began to tell myself, "I love this. This hurts, but I love it. I love the breeze through my armpits. I love the rain. I am a fucking badass." And that's the stuff I could believe.

I relied entirely on mindset to finish that race. Every time I thought about my husband, parents, kids, sister, and brother-in-law waiting for me at the finish line in the cold, wet rain, doubt crept in. So, I convinced myself that I loved this.

Mindset is key, but it can also gently slip into delusion. I sort of breached delusion during the marathon. No harm, though. I finished standing up and three minutes ahead of the eighty-four-year-old. But, afterwards, I was pretty sure I was not loving it and knew I never wanted to run another one.

But let's remain on the positive side of mindset. Tell better stories! Too many people believe the stories they are told, and then they go looking for reinforcement of those belief systems from the outside world. Remember the broken windshield? Recognize the possibility of radical change within yourself. Regulate and manage your inner work to affect your outer world.

Be aware of the types of stories you're already telling yourself. That ugly little voice inside your head often illuminates the path to expansion. One of my favorite authors, Martha Beck, put it beautifully:

> *Your worst suffering is your guide to tell you which belief you need to question.*

Sometimes choosing better stories means fighting the conscious mind. When the mystical happens, for example, oftentimes there is an overwhelming feeling of awe and connection, a certainty of one's place in this Universe. Then the ego feels the grip of control loosening and wakes up. It starts to doubt. It can't be; it was in my mind. This is the moment that you either believe what you have witnessed or experienced and allow yourself to change the story of what you've been taught, or you slip back into the ego again. Telling better stories and including the mystical parts of you takes bravery and faith in yourself.

It's no secret: You consciously or subconsciously choose the stories you want to live. Then you live them.

Exercises & Reflections:

Don't look at the future through the lens of the past. To tell better stories you need to know which stories you're currently telling. We create stories and pick up belief systems for every part of our lives so we will be referring to the Soul Centers for these exercises and reflections. Break out that workbook or journal and jot down the Soul Centers. Then for each area dive into the following:

1) *What are you currently telling yourself?* Start by reflecting on one Soul Center. For example, body. From there you can drill down deeper and break out each Soul Center: body image, strength, confidence in its ability to heal itself, etc.

   How do you speak to yourself about your body? What do you say? How does that make you feel when you tap into these beliefs?

2) *Does it serve you?* Does the story you are telling yourself bring you up or take you down? Take an honest look at how your beliefs make you feel, and if they aren't lifting you up, they're best left behind.

3) *Change your story.* This is where I blow your mind. You get to change your story. Yeah, that's right. If what you're telling yourself is bringing you down, rewrite the narrative. Don't lie to yourself; find a

way to shift the angle. This may mean you need to make some big changes in order to rewrite the story and remain in your truth. If you are telling yourself you're broke and can't make rent, telling yourself a different story isn't going to pay the bills. You may need to get another job and then live a different story. The shift in your beliefs may be, *I can get a better paying job, I am a valuable employee.*

Using your examples in #1, rewrite any negative stories.

4) *Having trouble releasing some of your old stories? Burn them up.* Fire ceremonies are very healing and can be simple. Write it on a slip of paper, hold the paper to your heart, and set the intention of releasing to the Universe all of the emotions and energetic ties.

Jeanine Tripodi

Chapter 5

Jeanine Tripodi

Secret #5:
Gather Your Tools

Use tools to remind yourself that you are a badass at life, that you're divinely connected, and that you hold the key to your own peace and purpose. You'll reach for these tools to tap back into the confidence and wisdom that comes with knowing your soul's voice and being in alignment with your higher Self. Your tools help you when your faith is shaken, but you still know you must trust yourself and your inner compass above all else.

Your tools are unique to you, and they shift as you grow. No person is always one thing or another. It's easy and expected that we slip into this filtered version of life, showing only the curated pieces to the public, but if you're totally honest with yourself, and then by default honest with the world around you, aren't you more complicated than that?

Embracing the many facets of your Self is to honor your truths. Honoring your soul like this, even when it goes against the grain of society, is what it means to be true to you.

I'm an enigma. A veritable paradox by definition.

I am a vegetarian who carries only leather bags. I'm a tree-hugging liberal who loves to shoot guns. I'm a spreader of peace, and I'd punch you in the throat if you really deserved it (like, really deserved it).

I like my things, and I like that you like your things, but your things don't have to be my things, and mine don't have to be yours. Freeing, isn't it?

And the things you like can be incongruent with some parts of you; they don't need to make sense to anyone else. Botox is one of my things, and it has made me a happier person—at least, that's what my kids think.

I'll be totally honest; if you ever told me that I'd be a fan of Botox, I probably would have slapped you sideways. I'd seen too many frozen expressions, botched facelifts, and horror stories to ever consider doing those things. But hey, never say never because in my experience that's the moment the Universe orchestrates some opportunity for you to see things in a new light. Look, I'm not trying to blame the Universe for my newfound appreciation of the big B. I'm just saying,

> if you're an open and willing participant of the cosmos who is ready and willing to expand your preconceived notions and opinions in an effort to create growth in your consciousness, and you take a hard line on something, you can expect to be bitch slapped.

So when my kids kept asking me why I was angry when I was having one of the most peaceful mornings of my existence, I realized that maybe my permanent brow-scowl was sending off the wrong messages.

After much thought, I told my husband that evening as I brushed my teeth with my homemade toothpaste that I was considering getting some Botox done. He started to laugh at me. "Pa-lease, you would never inject that into your body!"

I finished brushing.

"Yeah, why not?" I said as I began to oil pull the toxins from my gums with my organic coconut oil.

He shifted his eyes sideways, calculating his next expression. Sometimes, I think I like to keep him on his toes, always guessing, open to possibilities; not sure if

I'm coming or going. Or maybe I just wanted to get rid of my frowny face.

The next week I found a highly recommended dermatologist. Super professional. Perfect skin, not a wrinkle on her face. She was either really good at what she did, or she was twelve. She explained everything, and I was ready to roll. Nothing about it made me nervous; I was ready. She asked me if I had any concerns.

"Actually, one," I said. "I am Puerto Rican and Italian. I use a lot of facial expressions, and it's pretty imperative that I be able to give the Puerto Rican eye to my kids when we're at Target, or they won't know that I am reprimanding them when we are in public."

She assured me I'd keep my evil eye, and it would look natural. Sweet.

The gradual brow paralysis took about ten days to set in. Jared was obsessed with trying to see the transformation happen in real time. But, true to her word, it was gentle and natural, and guess what? My kids stopped asking what was wrong, and the mood in the house shifted just slightly.

OK, so what's the moral of the story here, and what does Botox have to do with tools to gather when shit goes sideways? Well, first, we are complex beings, so get ready to embrace the idea that some of the tools you use in your life may be peripheral and seem contradictory to some parts of you. And second, sometimes your tools just make you happy for the moment so you can redirect your attention and regroup, kinda like getting your mustache waxed. You go from feeling fuzzy and grubby to feeling fresh and youthful again. Complex, I know.

When shit does go sideways, though, I need to consciously remind myself to start with me. Ever since I was a kid, my first response to bad news or an uncertain situation is for my ears to feel like they are sliding back on my head, causing my head to tilt back just slightly, and then my ears seal closed to muffle the exterior sounds. A wave of pins and needles rolls from my forehead, across the top of my head, and down to my upper back. Simultaneously, my shoulders and collarbone shiver from the inside out, and my heart feels like a fifty-pound rock. At this point, I either run for my life, or hopefully in more cases than not, I try to remember to pull myself in and ground myself.

Shed the panic and breathe.

Breathing really is the first step. I've never held my breath until passing out, but I have seen someone who did, and voluntarily. Now, that was messed up. It's a natural response to close up, shut down, and look outside for answers. The challenge is remembering to turn to your Self first. It helps when you live in authenticity.

Soulful authenticity is your most valuable tool if you really want to catapult your own growth, help others, and remember where you stand when shit goes sideways. I have been to more than one self-empowering conference where the speaker talked about being authentic and sharing our stories. It's all true. All of it. But telling your story, whether it's to yourself or others, isn't enough. You have to dive so fucking deep into your Self that the earth shakes beneath you.

Being authentic means being brutally honest with yourself. You must be willing to dig into your stories with compassion and then cull the diamonds from the dirt. Be vulnerable. Expose yourself so completely that when you do share your truths, they are so purely you, it no longer matters what anyone else thinks or believes because there is no other reality. You stop seeking their approval or permission. You take responsibility for yourself.

When you get brave enough to look into the dark corners of your experiences, you find the place where you can access the light. It's that light that becomes the lighthouse for yourself and for others.

I had been practicing energetic healing for more than a decade before I stepped into my full authenticity. When

I started my practice, it was small and just OK. I felt frustrated and like I was half-assing things. When I dove into my soulful authenticity, everything changed, from how I helped women to what I created, to understanding what I was really pissed about.

For many years my practice was a side passion. I served others through one-on-one energy and hypnosis sessions, delivering the tools I was taught within the framework of my mentors. My sessions were great, but I constantly felt like I was holding something back. It was frustrating and unsettling. In meditation, I regularly asked myself how I could best help my tribe. I didn't have answers right away, but I knew they would come when I was ready. I'm not super good at patience.

About eight months after I really started looking for these answers, it hit me all at once during a meditation: I had been playing small all these years, and the hard truth was that that had been my own choice. I think I kept my practice limited so I didn't have to go through the soul-centered work to unearth the diamonds I was really meant to share with the world. Instead of diving in, I kept my sessions conservative, helping people with smoking cessation and other socially acceptable, mainstream, everyday challenges. I put my attention into supportive roles for my husband's businesses. I avoided the light in my own stories because it took a level of raw authenticity I wasn't prepared to share. It also took a whole lot of self-confidence, and no matter how confident I thought I was, I often shied from sharing my metaphysical experiences too deeply.

I realized that what I was really pissed about was that I hadn't stepped into my own path earlier. I was pissed that I waited so long to believe in myself enough to build my programs. That was the moment I was finally ready to jump into the authenticity of my stories without fear of how others would receive them and start the book I had wanted to write for the past twelve years. The process opened up the way I hold my sessions, work with women, and teach my programs. My tribe responded and my lighthouse shined. My authenticity was in my truths, unfiltered by the truths held by those around me.

Until I began teaching through my own authentic experiences and views of the nonphysical, I was giving only 40 percent of myself at best. Now, I strive to play big and accept that I'm not for everyone. That smells less like disapproval and more like freedom to me now. I am not everyone's cup of tea. It's liberating.

Realizing this and putting more faith in my own truths keeps me rooted in my soul. When I'm not rooted, I flail and have to remind myself of my tools and these secrets. We're all human; we're not supposed to get it all right all the time. There's zero growth in that. When crisis hits, be aware of knee-jerk reactions to run outside of yourself for assurance and confidence. Listen to the external input, sure, but don't forget to keep your hands on the wheel. Keep driving, don't lose sight of your truths. Yes, reach out for help when you need it, we all need help. We came here to help each other grow, but turn to your Self first.

So besides Botox and soulful authenticity, what are my favorite go-to tools? Clean eating, exercise, tribe, Reiki, gratitude, meditation, and intuition. Not necessarily in that order and not totally complete. I may want that Häagen-Dazs first.

I have a workout partner and a trainer who let me text pictures of my meals to them. I don't do it all the time because, you know, pizza night, but it is helpful to have that accountability when I find myself careening off course. They're part of my tribe.

Clean eating and exercise are two of my tools that really keep me centered and grounded. In fact, if I am totally honest, when I am eating too much crap, I feel fairly disconnected from my physical body and nonphysical self. It was really just this past year that I comprehended the profound affect eating clean has on my spirituality and balance. I have to thank my trainer for this one. He's twenty-four and wicked smart, one of these next-generation humans who is intelligent and actively conscious. He is naturally in tune with his higher Self and is better read at twenty-four than I am at forty-eight. And damn it if he doesn't remind me on the daily how much clearer I am when I focus on fueling myself well. Find what works for you and surround yourself with people who support you.

Tribe is important.

Don't feel like you have one? Not inspired by yours? Find a new one; it's that important. We are naturally inclined to travel this life in packs. Make sure yours has your back and is moving in the same direction you want to go.

Keep in mind that your larger tribe often has many sub-tribes, such as one that supports your forward growth in business, another for emotional support, and another to lean on when times are sad. You get the idea.

Find your tribe
and know that,
like everything,
your tribe
will change
as you do.

This can be a hard truth to swallow, especially if you're going through a major life change or loss or if you have had to cling to your tribe for survival. During the depths of our despair after Max died, we faced this reality a few times. Tribes change.

When I found out I was pregnant with Max, I couldn't wait to run across the street to share the news with my best friend. Just weeks before, she had announced she was expecting her second child and, knowing that we were trying, she had commented about how fun it would be to be pregnant together. It was. We did water aerobics, took walks, and went baby clothes shopping, all with our two-year-old daughters in tow. We imagined the four of them growing up together, BBQs, school, vacations, and so on.

She was a great addition to my tribe. She was fun and creative, and our husbands were also good friends. When her son arrived in mid-October, we celebrated his arrival. I couldn't wait to bring Max into the world. We'd walk and talk and help each other get through that first year of diapers and sleep deprivation. Then two weeks later, Max came. And he left.

I would be remiss if I didn't say she tried to remain a part of my tribe, at least at first. Consumed by my own grief, I didn't allow myself to imagine how difficult it was for her. It is only now, twelve years later, that it occurs to me perhaps she imagined me crying in Max's empty room as she rocked her baby to sleep just across the street. I don't know. We stopped talking.

During grief group, there was a lot of talk about how it felt to have friends and family pregnant, with newborns, making baby announcements, and celebrating milestone birthdays. Some of my grief group friends felt rage and anger. They didn't want to be around pregnant women or were offended to be invited to gatherings. I understood those responses, but I didn't feel the same. While I don't think I could have held myself together at a baby shower, I did want to separate my story from other pregnant women's. I wanted to see new life, to feel hope.

I would have loved to have held her son more. I would have loved to have seen him grow, to observe the differences between girls and boys. He was a marker of where Max would be in life. As she undoubtedly struggled through her first year with her new family, she tried to support me. She offered to watch my toddler while I saw my therapist or went to Pilates. I should have known it was too much.

I don't know when it began or how it bubbled up, but it ended with me screaming back at her on the phone while collapsing to the floor in my master closet. She complained about my not understanding her pain, about the audacity of my accepting her offers of help, there was more, I can't even remember. "Your heart," I told her, "is a cold fucking stone."

We tried to make up once, but I couldn't move beyond the things she said. I wasn't capable of understanding how this all played out for her, and I don't think she had the capacity to hold any part of me. We didn't drag the goodbye out; it felt better to just accept that we couldn't salvage the friendship. It was freeing not to be angry. Tribes change, and it's OK. We can only give what we can give.

Reiki is one of the first places I turn when I need to regain my footing. It centers me, connects me to my Universe, and brings me back to my heart center. When I am in this centered place, the doors of gratitude crack open. I then direct my focus on gratitude into different areas of my life, which raises my vibrational signal. Sometimes I will think to myself about what I'm grateful for, and other times I will write it in a journal. However you choose to bring your focus to gratitude, be sure you are getting specific. Being general with things like, "I'm grateful for my health," is nice, but they lose the punch of the specific emotion. Instead try, "I'm grateful that my body is strong and allows me to play and run around with my children." It paints a more meaningful picture for your conscious and subconscious minds and one that more easily generates the feeling that goes with these thoughts.

Remember, your vibrational signal is generated by the energy of your feelings. When I get specific and focus on gratitude, I can begin to re-regulate my emotions and subsequently my responses to life. You can't control much in life, but you can control your responses. This includes deciding how long you will stay in anger, how quickly you will choose action over paralysis, and exactly how much you will allow your ego to internalize before deciding to draw into your own strength and take that next step forward. Choosing to regulate your emotions ultimately lays out the path to navigate when shit goes sideways.

Meditation helps me regulate my emotions and responses, too. I often bring up meditation with my clients. Some have told me they have tried to meditate but can't make their mind go blank or they say they feel like if they can't do it for thirty minutes a day, every day, they're failing. Let's be clear here; this isn't failing, and I don't know anyone who can stop their mind and create a blank space. Five minutes is better than no minutes.

I would love to tell you I meditate every day, but that would be a lie, and I am big into honesty. We are humans with lots of shit going on, so if you can meditate for twenty minutes one day and then only ninety seconds in the shower another day, I am still going to say you are a badass. Meditation is when you close the door to the past and future and remain only in this moment in time. It takes practice. Some days, you're gonna nail it, and others, you're going to fidget until you get up for a cup of coffee. Don't judge yourself.

Of all of the tools I have discussed, none is as important as my intuition. Without it, I feel wholly disconnected. There have been times when I have ignored my intuition, not noticed it, and even allowed someone else to discourage me from believing it. In hindsight, every single time, I wish I had trusted myself above all else. Gather your tools and fine-tune them, but always lean into your inner wisdom. You were born with this inner compass; let it guide you. Does this mean you should never run it through the filter of your conscious mind? No. But listen first and then decide what to do with the information.

Let's talk a little bit about control. It used to be my favorite go-to. I thought it was a tool, but it really turned out to be an illusion. I was not alone in the pursuit of control. The more I spoke with people about their tools for managing life's chaos, the more I heard people try to reach for control. Stop everything, grab firm, and force. Make it happen. Make them do it.

Here's the thing: it doesn't work, and it pushes you farther away from your source. Control is human; it's the ego, really. We are hard-wired to control our environment, each other, the outcome, the game, and the rules. Then we win, right? I used to think so. It felt good to control, to manipulate and negotiate for a desirable outcome, to finesse, to chart a course and force the mold. But when you transcend that human compulsion, when you rise above that picture you've so emphatically painted, you realize there is no such thing.

We have zero control, especially when it comes to change, and change is the way to newness and more.

It takes most of us some pretty life-altering experiences to see and accept this. But when you do, when you can feel the truth of it fill your weakened, battered body, you've transcended control, and you've accessed connection to what's above.

Loosen the grip. It makes the inevitable change easier to flow along with. Less resistance, more sway.

It's in our nature to hold tightly to the things we love or want or need, but change is inevitable and far less painful when we aren't gripping so damn tightly.

I remember telling a spiritual advisor that parenting my children when they were babies often felt like I was the eagle with talons gripping my young so strongly that I had to be careful not to pierce their soft skin. It wasn't a good feeling: protection teetering on destruction. Well, maybe "destruction" is extreme, but you get it. My fear was not being able to save them, to help them, to carry them all out of the fiery plane crash or the sinking ship or the—Dear God, there are four of them! My real issue was control, and this kind of thinking breeds fear and the need for more control.

Losing our son Max certainly fed fears into this need to keep my other four kids safe, but my thoughts and feelings on the matter never made me feel better, and I'm sure the vibe I was throwing off wasn't making the kids feel better either.

I was reminded that ultimately we have no control. Control is an illusion, and for those who are reading this right now and feeling a rise of anger calling "bullshit," I say to you, I get it, I really do. I used to feel that way too, and it's still an illusion. We can only navigate this world with intention, desire, and focus and be open to learning from all the turns. Breathe. Let your shoulders drop. Feel your connection to the earth and the sky and lead from your heart. The rest falls into place.

It wasn't until I loosened my grip that I was able to trust more. Trust that things would be OK. Trust that each of my children have their own connection with the Universe. Trust that feelings of fear and control don't lead to feelings of freedom and safety. When I visualized releasing my talons, I let guilt and fear slip though my grasp.

Loosen your grip. That inevitable change that's peeking around the corner is coming, and when your grip is loose and flexible, you'll flow through it all without as many blisters and calluses.

A note about tools when navigating mental health

If you are having mental health issues or a crisis, read this twice. Please don't try to go it alone. Get professional help. This is not the time to try to muscle through. When our souls chose to come to this physical world, we chose to migrate in soul circles because we came to help each other. So, reach out, call for professional help. Yes, we all have our own connections to the divine, but we also came here to raise our vibrations together and to support each other in our growth.

If you are having dark, suicidal thoughts, put this book down and call The National Suicide Prevention Hotline at 1-800-273-8255.

Also, your higher Self, your guides, teachers, angels, and intuition are all always positive. You will never hear or feel guidance or direction to harm yourself or others. Your divine support system only works in light and love, and if you're experiencing anything other than that, you need to see a professional for help.

I will not mince words: you deserve to feel love and self-value. Get professional help.

In times of my deepest sorrow, strangers have brought some of the brightest light to me. Reach out. Ask for help.

It's no secret: Even a badass, spiritual gangsta like you needs a reservoir of support to reach for when shit goes sideways.

I asked thousands of women what they reach for when shit goes sideways, and here is what they landed on:

Sour Dinosaurs, every time. Meditation. Heavy lifting. Madonna. Journaling. Gratitude. Reiki. Acupuncture. Chocolate. Dancing. Jump squats. Yoga. Crying. Cleaning my house. Pedicures. Cheetos. Handstands. 80s music. Country music. Deep breathing. Work out. Laundry. Time with friends. Time with family. A good book. A pint of Häagen-Dazs. A run. A hike. Playing guitar. Rest. Walks. Remind myself I haven't picked up a bottle in seven years. Time with my dogs. Shower. Bath. Tea. Manicure. Massage. Haircut. A chat with the ocean. Ice cream. Reminding myself that I have nothing to be ashamed of when I eat "crap." Gratitude. Walks alone in nature. Listening to the beautiful sounds in nature. Aromatherapy. Sugar cookies. Beach walks. Art. Sunset. Shopping. Discard many items off my to-do list. Take naps. Painting. Singing. Praying. Asking myself "What is the next logical step?" Baskin-Robbins. I look at a picture of me at age three smiling. Cuss a lot. Podcasts. Laying in the sun. Vent session with a friend. Write a 'feel good' journal and pull it out to remind myself of the good things that feel good. Therapy. A latte. Epsom salt bath. Creating art. Netflix binging. Coffee with a friend. CBD. A green patch of grass to lay on. Getting my hands dirty with art. I meditate over my paintings and say, "Hell, I created this!." I drive around for thirty minutes. Breathe and voice a positive out loud. A long warm bath. Gratitude. Appreciation. Love.

Exercises & Reflections:

Find your tools, gather them, and create a supportive love-arsenal. Maybe you paint, and that muse cracks the door to enlightenment. Maybe baking a triple layer cake smells like empowerment to you. Recognize the tools you currently have, discern which are helpful and which keep you down, and identify new tools.

1) *What are your current tools?* Review the Soul Centers you have reflected on in previous chapters and next to each, list the tools you access when things get tough.

2) *Helping or hurting?* Next, decide which tools help lift you up and which tools are less than enlightening. Keep the former; let go of the latter.

3) *How would you like your tools to help you feel?* As you begin to consider adding more tools to your love-arsenal, think about how you'd like to feel. Ice cream is awesome, but does it give you a belly ache afterwards? If so, you may want to feel more than momentary comfort. Listing out the feelings that you're searching for especially in times of challenge will help you navigate back to center faster.

Chapter 6

Jeanine Tripodi

Secret #6:
Ask for Help

A lot has transpired since I started getting serious about writing this book. I already mentioned that, within the first few months of writing, we had a major financial crisis. I found myself reaching for just these steps of survival during that time. My work was validated as these Secrets helped me to navigate yet another bump in my road. I thanked the Universe out loud for allowing me to live my message and write this work in raw authenticity.

Toward the end of the writing of this book, I found myself, once again, charting a course through grief and loss with the end of my nineteen-year marriage.

Deciding it was time to end the marriage was difficult. We had four young children, and we had already survived so much in our time together. Many people in our tribe thought that our past record of survival meant that we should persevere. This pressure, coming from some of those closest to us, fostered uncertainty and caused me to doubt my inner knowing.

My intuition bubbled up many times, but I was confused because it conflicted with how I had consciously decided life should flow. I was supposed to partner with my husband and take on all of life's twists and turns with him. When it was clear to me life was unfolding differently from how I'd imagined and I had to make some decisions about how I wanted to live this life, I really focused on practicing Secret #6; I asked for help.

While I found a good therapist and spoke with a few close confidantes, answers didn't come until I sat in my own wisdom. I got serious and consistent about asking my guides and my higher Self for clarity, and that's when things shifted.

Throughout the day, I placed my hand over my heart chakra and set the intention of exuding compassion to everyone around me and myself. Every night before bed, I placed one hand over my heart and the other over my solar chakra and asked for clarity. I tried to keep my conscious mind quiet and avoided making up scenarios or allowing my mind to conjure up old hurts or disappointments. I detached from anger, sadness, and joy, and just asked for clarity.

Over the following several weeks, it was as if the film had been removed from my eyes. I was able to see things as they truly were. I had removed the clouded lenses I had been wearing. Answers surfaced, and perhaps most important, I was certain about my next steps even though I didn't know exactly where they would lead. I had faith that this was the road to take, and that it would ultimately be best for everyone involved, even though initially it would hurt us all.

Change is not usually comfortable.
But nothing changes if nothing changes.

Let me be clear. This life change didn't happen in a few weeks. It was a decade in the making, but clarity came fast when I cleared out the ego and external expectations.

You can ask for help from both your nonphysical and physical team. I am going to start this Secret with stories from the nonphysical, not because I hang out there more often, but because a lot of you reading this have experienced a whole lot of nonphysical connections but haven't had the validation from someone saying to you, "I get it; something like that has happened to me too; that makes sense; trust it; I don't think that's coincidence. I think that's a sign. How did it feel? Trust that."

Babe, I am that voice for you.

Asking your nonphysical team for help

Ask them quietly in prayer, scream from the mountaintop, wail out loud during therapy; just ask. Then listen. (Listen = feel = observe = believe = be open = trust = truth.)

Each question you ask opens doors for you; your guides and teachers are there to help. Guides are experts in certain areas and will offer you consult, whereas teachers will assist you through the learning experiences you choose. You have to ask the questions and be present for the answers. No guide or teacher will do it for you. You ask the questions, you make the decisions, and you do the work. But having the guidance helps you to make the choices that best suit your soul's purpose. There is no right or wrong way to do this life. There are different paths; some are easier, some more difficult, and some are more enjoyable, and when you get out of your own way by releasing the ego and communing with your higher Self and your divine support team, you have access to more clearly marked paths of joy.

Ask to see clearly.
Listen to your dreams.
Release control and be open to what comes up.

When I am going through a tough time, I try to avoid asking for specific outcomes. Instead, I ask for clarity and confidence in my next steps. I ask for signs that I am on the right track. I ask to be sent opportunities to help me find my light. I ask for faith in all that I can't see but know is there.

We are wired to try to control our environment and the outcomes. We have been led to believe that this keeps us safe, but it doesn't work. Unfortunately, oftentimes we think we know exactly what we want and so we charge, with such narrow focus, toward an end goal and we end up missing all the beauty along the way. And what if that end goal isn't what the soul is really seeking? What if the purpose of the end goal is just to get us on the right path to something else?

Ask for help and be open to what shows up for you. It may be a person, or an opportunity, or a new way of seeing or feeling about something. Help can come in very tangible forms, but it can also create subtle shifts in your energy body.

Ask your divine support system for guidance. They will allow you to see opportunities for growth that have been there all along, but you must take the step and choose to see and act on them. You know, it's free will.

Write a message on a piece of paper and burn it to release it to the heavens.

Your guides and the Universe connect directly with your higher Self, your subconscious. Relax your brain and open up your awareness, allowing your attention to be redirected. That's your subconscious showing you the way and drawing attention to things that trigger trains of thought or action. Go with it. Stop questioning it. If it feels right, lean the fuck in. The messages aren't always what you'd expect, but they'll always offer insight if you're ready to hear them.

Spoiler alert: We don't always know exactly how it is supposed to turn out.

What?
Yeah. #Truth.

We all have our own experiences, and I am not here to tell you what to think or feel about the Universe around you. I am here to help you see what is already in front of you, to give you permission to listen to that positive and hopeful voice inside your head.

This isn't about telling you what *is*. It's about telling you that you are not crazy. That's your team rooting for you, guiding you. We all have one. Some call them angels; my grandmother used to call them my guardian angels.

We all have our own divine support system. Meet them. Ask them for guidance. They are here to help you.

It begs to be said again: your team will never tell you to hurt yourself or others. This team is strictly operating for your highest good. However, they also cannot override free will, and they won't rob you of an experience that would lend to your learning. And yeah, sometimes the experience isn't pleasant, and sometimes you wonder how there could possibly be a lesson or a shred of light to what's happening. I know, I have wondered.

My son died. How could there be any light in this?

This is the physical world; there is birth, life, and death, but maybe these stages aren't as separate as we like to think. Consider that the ways we see the beginning and the end may only mark the intersections of soul and body on earth. Maybe we signed up for all of the contrast when we chose to come into these physical bodies. I have been shown that there are lessons in the pain.

A month after Max died, I was at home lying in bed. We had shut down our business and taken an indefinite amount of time off. My mother had just left for home. More emptiness. She had this way of being present and invisible at the same time. She let me unravel. She picked up where I had just stopped: feeding Simone, cleaning my house. I was a ghost myself, and I expect there were times while I slept that she checked to be sure I was still breathing.

It was early, the sun was up, but the streets were quiet. Any grieving person will tell you that this is the worst time of day. There is a moment as you awake when you draw that slow, deep breath and gently open your eyes to the dawn of a new day, and, just for a second, you forget that you're broken. Just for that millisecond, you feel normal. Then a rush of pain and chaos, a wave of grief crashes down with such force, you gasp for breath. And then comes guilt. You feel guilt that your mind or your soul or your brain could betray you like this, betray your son. It's a blessing and a curse.

Nope. It's just a fucking curse.

Jared was in the shower. I could hear it running. I felt like my body was physically sinking into the bed. I actually felt true fear that my body was somehow going to submerge inside the fibers of the mattress. For a moment, I began to doubt the physics of matter. I know it doesn't make sense logically, but not much did at this time, and I fully expected to see the mattress creep up into my peripheral vision and envelop me like quicksand. The thought was both terrifying and inviting.

Up until this point I had never yelled at God. After all, I didn't have many conversations with Him. I talked with Crow and the wind and the trees and my dead ancestors. I never asked why because I knew deep inside that was a meaningless question. When I thought about the flow of events, by which I mean the flow of the soul, not the medical steps, I floated in this ethereal space of observation. As if I were suspended, no longer needing air to fill my lungs, I was simply observing and seeing in my mind's eye.

So, as I lay there, I relived hearing friends and family entertain the question of why. Some skipped the why and went straight to rationalizing all the reasons why God needed another angel or that next time my baby would live because, "How could this happen again?" (A note to anyone supporting a griever: as well-meaning as you are, I'd bet less on these words bringing comfort and more on the possibility of receiving a throat punch.)

And so I lay there, barely breathing, feeling like my shallow slow breaths barely fed enough oxygen to my heart and not too sure I cared if they did. I began to wonder if I should ask why. Before this thought finished crossing my mind, I heard and felt and knew this rush of a voice I had heard before in the hospital. She simply said, "WHY NOT?"

And in that same overlapping instant I saw a flash of imagery like a clip reel from *National Geographic*, moving faster and faster with each image: a lioness licking her dead cub and roaring to the stars, a landslide in a far-off country where a woman wept with her hands over her face and the bodies of her five children muddied and laid out at her feet. I saw death on a highway. Entire families wiped out in war. I watched a pioneer mother bury her daughter on the Oregon Trail. I saw blurred imagery moving so fast, and I knew that death was part of life. It wasn't separate. It wasn't even different. It was a part of it all.

This reel of imagery, it didn't leave me with feeling of "It could be worse" or "Count your blessings." It left me knowing and grounded, almost settled in the understanding that death isn't the end; it is quite simply part of the flow.

I am not going to tell you that this moment launched me out of my grief. It did not. I still felt deep and weighted loss, but I knew that WHY wasn't a question that would bring me any closer to understanding or acceptance or resolve.

Asking WHY was searching for meaning outside.

Tears streamed silently down my face, soaking my pillow. Jared's shower was still running. I felt desperately alone. At the hospital, her voice guided me; here, she shed light on death.

I needed more. I wanted to feel my spirit guides. Hairs stood up on my upper neck, and a wave of worry that they weren't around me washed over me. So, with guilt and shame for doubting their presence when so many times throughout my life they've passed my tests of validation and requests for signs, I asked, "Guides, if you are with me, please, please give me a sign, and I'm sorry that I have to ask. I know you're here, but I can't feel you. I feel nothing. My body is cold from the inside out. Please show me a sign. Let me feel your presence."

I have tried to explain what happened next for the past thirteen years. Without being inside my body, I'm not sure anyone can grasp its wholeness. Simultaneously, time froze, as if the physical plane had been paused and all sounds were nonexistent, all except a very loud, thick, and consistent buzzing sound, as if I were standing inside electricity itself.

I felt a presence along my spine that wrapped around me like arms and weighted wings, completely encasing me. At the rate with which I drew my breaths, these arms slowly squeezed me three times, and with each firm squeeze, the buzzing sound expanded. I felt, in every cell of my body, a sensation that I can only describe as pure love.

While feeling all of this, I viewed my body from a bird's-eye perspective and saw the entire form as a 3-D grid; all the lines connected with small circles at the joints. I looked like a 3-D model of the children's toy, K'Nex, all blue, and with each squeeze, every single section and joint lit up to a brilliant blue color. It was the most incredible experience of my life, and nothing has been the same since. I gained a new understanding of etheric energy, the ways in which we can connect, and the subtle yet powerful support system available to us all.

Tune into the signs that show up outside of your body as well. Environmental signs can show up in countless ways. A meaningful song playing at just the right moment. The smell of perfume. Noticing repeating numbers. Driving under a street sign that literally gives you an answer. Seeing the face of someone you know in that of a stranger passing by. Coincidence? Your subconscious? Your subconscious is the same as your higher Self. Why wouldn't our higher Self, our guides, and our angels communicate through the most direct channels and in the easiest ways? It's affirming to receive validation or nudges when the communication is undeniable, but it is common for the messages to come through more subtly.

I get asked by my clients a lot, "Hey, do you think that this was a sign?" And my response is always, "If you think it's a sign, it's probably a sign."

A few months after Matilda was born, I was sitting on my back patio contemplating life and death and what makes us set different types of limits on ourselves. I thought about running. I was a track runner in high school and loved sprints but detested anything longer than a 400 meter. I had trained for years and had never gone farther than four miles. I decided in that moment that I could run five miles if I decided to. In fact, I could run a marathon if I wanted. The idea was exciting. It was crazy! I had to do it but had no idea how.

Before I even put my drink back down on the table, and this is no exaggeration, the mailman knocked on the side fence (which he never did) and hand-delivered the mail (which he never did). On top of the pile was an invitation from a charity that trains participants to run the Portland marathon in exchange for charity fundraising. The meeting to sign up was that night within three hours. I took this as a clear sign to get off my ass and run a marathon.

Your guides and your divine support system will show up for you when you ask. During the months after Max's death, Grandma Tripodi made her presence and support known. I woke up one day and felt a compulsion to bake anise seed biscotti, to sew, and to paint every single day for months. This was not like me —well, maybe the baking, but I had never painted before, and I always opted for iron-on Stitch Witchery instead of sewing. This was definitely Grandma Tripodi hanging around, and I was sure of it when I smelled her perfume and cigarettes.

Whenever I sat on the orange couch to check out and pass time in front of the TV, I would feel my dog, Yukon's, presence. I would smell him and feel a tickle of his long hair under my nose and on my face. Sometimes, it was so palpable, I would have to vigorously rub my hands over my face to get rid of the feeling. And whenever we spoke about Max, he let us know he was around by turning on and off the TV and flicking lights on and off.

In later years after Cagui passed, I saw his face in the face of a passing stranger. His image was so clear. I knew it was his way of "shapeshifting" the stranger's face to show me he was there with me. My grandmother, Abu, also visited this way often. I was walking down Hawthorne Street in Portland when I smelled her perfume, only to look up and see her face smile at me through a woman walking by. Oftentimes these visits came on or around significant dates or anniversaries. I told one skeptic about this encounter, and he was certain it was merely my subconscious mind. Since I believe the subconscious is an extension of the higher Self, which is an extension of the Universe that connects the consciousness of us all, I guess I'm cool with that.

Then there are the times when you get to share a visitation sign with someone. Those are fun times. On one particularly emotional day, I was driving to preschool, and while staring at the beautiful Oregon sky, I told Max I felt alone and asked him to show me a sign that he was with me. I shuffled the kids into their classrooms and walked out with my friend heading for coffee. In the midst of the chaos in the hallway, there was a brand-new little baby in a carrier.

For a split-second my friend and I thought he was alone, but then his mother stepped over to pick him up. He was the most glowing baby I had seen, and I was moved to tell her aloud how incredibly beautiful he was. I was probably bordering on seeming a little weird with my gushing over this baby, and so we walked off. Halfway down the hall, I found myself asking without even registering that the words were pouring from my mouth, "What is his name?"

She replied, "Maximus."

I looked at my friend and tears welled in both of our eyes. She simply said, "I heard it, too."

You see, my Max was also a Maximus, and while I had met a Max and a Maxwell, I had yet to meet another

Maximus. If ever I doubted this visit, my friend was there to remind me she felt it too.

You can ask them to stay and you can ask them to leave.

I made this mistake after being startled by an energy in my home. Alone in my house, I was walking up the stairs when I felt this rush of energy. It startled me so much, I put my hand out behind me and impulsively yelled, "Leave!" In an instant it was gone, and the air felt empty and still. I didn't mind at the time and actually felt relief, then went about my day.

It was a good nine months of wondering why I felt so alone and why I couldn't feel my ancestors around me before I recalled inadvertently asking *all* energy to leave.

So how do you ask your divine team for help?

Ask. Listen. Trust.

There is no wrong way to ask your guides for help. Remember, it all comes from your intention. But for those of you who are Type A (like me) or just want more guidance and rules, read on. I get you, and I got you.

I find it helpful to take some time and space to connect. This can be as complicated as a ceremony with candle lighting, music, drumming, incense burning, and intention setting or as simple as a deep breath and a focused heart. Taking a few deep breaths and centering and grounding myself brings me to a calm place where I can ask for clarity of next steps without piling on all the garbage flooding my mind at that moment. The fastest way I center and ground is to visualize a column of light flowing from the universe into the crown of my head, filling my body, and expanding around me and down through the earth. And then I ask.

I ask my guides and divine support system for guidance and clarity: "Help me to see, hear, feel, and know what I need exactly at this moment."

And then I wait, listen, and observe. Sometimes signs come quickly, and sometimes it's more indirect. Soften your gaze; allow your subconscious and higher Self to expand and your conscious mind to quiet. Think with your body and energy system, not just your brain. Be open. Aware. Don't doubt. Refer to Secret #3, Tap Into the Voice of Your Soul.

As we discussed before, don't sweat trying to figure out if it's a sign. If you think it's sign, it's a sign. And if it gets you thinking or leaning in a direction, lean in. But also check in. Does it feel good? Does it feel right? Are you feeling settled? That's when you know. When it feels like an antacid has been tossed on a glass full of bubbly acid, that's when you know you're on track. Clarity can feel scary but also right. It isn't about avoiding the pain, it's about walking through the fire because you know it's the way out.

Asking your physical team for help

This is where your tribe comes in. I hope you got serious about Secret #5, Gather Your Tools, because this is where you ask them for help. Reach for your tools.

Connect with your tribe and start diving into your tools. Reach for the ones that resonate today and that may change tomorrow. Be flexible and open. Think of asking for help like it's an all-you-can-eat buffet. You walk down the line, picking and choosing what looks good, and when you feel like trying something else, you get a new plate.

My biggest advice here is to remember to ask for help. No one knows what you need and want until you tell them. So between pints of Ben & Jerry's, take that bath, call your confidante, and tap into your tools.

Whether you are asking for help in the nonphysical or physical world, letting go and not looking for a specific answer is the fastest way to find what you're looking for. When you surrender the feelings behind what you're seeking and let go of any feelings attached to the conflict or problem, you allow for solutions you never even considered. You free up the universe to deliver infinite possibilities.

It's no secret: Chances are your friends aren't mind readers, and your divine support system respects free will. You gotta *ask*.

Exercises & Reflections:

Asking for help can be difficult for some but it's time to get over that. Remember, we have come to this lifetime in soul circles with the intention of helping each other grow and expand but we are also human.

Your friend has her kids, a sick in-law, and a job. She may not know you need her support. Your divine support team will wait until they're asked to ensure your free will. So the first step in asking for help is asking for help.

1) *What has worked in the past?* Different Soul Centers require different kinds of help. Reflect on all of your identified Soul Centers and for each one, journal about a time when you asked for help. What did you ask for and how did it help?

2) *Connect with your nonphysical support team.* Meditate with the intention of connecting and asking for guidance. Then wait and observe. The signs that you notice are meant for you.

3) *Reach out to your tribe.* Sometimes, when we are in the moment when shit is going sideways, we forget that we have a rich tribe of support. For each Soul Center area, list in your journal people, groups and organizations in your tribe who would be your go-to for help.

Chapter 7

Jeanine Tripodi

Secret #7:
Choose Joy

Choose joy in the midst of chaos.
Choose love.
Choose yourself.

Regrets are bitter. I am honey.

Regret is both complicated and yet so very simple, and like every emotion, it's your choice. In my experience, any time I dabbled in big regret I suffered deeply. After all, what is regret but an emotional response to trigger guilt and sadness while emotionally whipping yourself for the choices or actions of the past? You can't change them, and no amount of guilt will alleviate suffering. Regret and guilt are the dark pits of despair. This isn't to say that a whiff of regret can't be beneficial; if used correctly, it can cause you to course correct your future. But your past? That ship has sailed, sister. Make amends. Change your actions. Do better next time. Stand up for yourself. Pay your dues. Just move on.

If I am totally honest, I do allow myself to regret the little and medium things. I regret when I eat too many handfuls of chocolate. I regret when I stay up until 2 a.m., surfing the internet. I regret not letting my dog, Marvin, out to pee before bed. Those are impulse choices that are annoying but don't warrant any level of emotional frequency. They're like the meh of regrets. Whatevs.

I do, however, consciously choose to let go of the big regrets. It's not like I haven't made some regrettable choices, like moving across the country with no job prospect, not confronting the elephant in the room earlier, allowing my life to unravel in ways that led me straight into bankruptcy, acquiescing to some big decisions even when my intuition screamed at me not to because it was too uncomfortable to assert my truths.

I try to remind myself not to regret because these are the steps that got me here today in this moment. And here is the place from which I'll take my next steps forward.

Regret is a funny thing. When people regret and wish they could do over, they're assuming that a different choice would lead to a different result. Maybe. Or maybe it's all about the journey and not the landing spot. I mean, really, next week today's landing spot, from which I launch my next step, is merely a stone on the path to where I am headed.

Joy exists even when shit goes sideways, but choosing joy doesn't mean opting for denial. There will be times when you simply need to tread in the darker waters for a bit. Just trust that while joy may be hiding for a time, if you maintain the faith that your journey will continue to flow, it will surface for you again. When it does, just like the lotus blooming from the murky waters, it will bring forth beauty in the darkness.

As you move through the shit, recognize that you can choose joy even if it's in pieces. You can choose hope even if hope is simply that the wave of pain rolls in a little more slowly or with less force. Baby steps.

Living the Secrets means accepting what is, trusting the journey, and making choices from the heart. And when things get stagnant, dive in, dig for more, and make waves in the murky waters. Are there days when you just need to dwell in the shitty waters of it all? Sure, but be aware of how long you tread water. When shit goes sideways, I give myself a period of time to accept feeling like crap without trying to move too quickly through it. It's important to feel and acknowledge the emotions and the stages. If I am unrealistic in this time estimation—*I have been known to try to fast track pretty much everything once I recognize what I'm dealing with*—I will reevaluate and allow for changes. Less structure, more gentle guidance. You get it.

If I don't keep a softly focused eye on the process and flow, I could easily slip into an abyss of timelessness. And if I don't encourage myself to make choices at some point—*and the timing of this is all up to us and maybe input from a good therapist or spiritual guide*—I could find myself sprawled on my couch, twisted up in blankets, smelling of stale chips and misery, watching reruns of Good Witch, eating day-old takeout, evaluating the strength of the plastic knife against my chest. Perhaps that's a bit dramatic, the knife part, but it sets the scene.

Choose joy even if it's in pieces.

The human urge is to control—control the process, the outcome, and the resolution. Control also surfaces in more subtle ways, like being certain that you know exactly what will give you joy and how to get it. But what happens when you get that thing you're chasing, and it doesn't yield the feelings you expected? What happens when the win still feels empty? The majority of us instinctively reach for more.

When faced with challenges, it's natural to try to map the way out and target an end goal in the hopes that it will bring you what you want. There is a sense of control in consciously predetermining how it should be. We all do it. But what if, in your conscious-driven roadmap, you forget to ease up on the forcing of things and miss out on the feeling of what you're really after?

Living the Secrets means being open to the distinct possibility that you don't really have the answers because each step builds to the next and reveals itself only when you are ready to see it. Trusting yourself and the Universe means enjoying that the journey may lead to unexpected places. Those places just may offer more joy than you could ever have imagined yourself. You will only find those places when you are ready to loosen the grip and trust in the flow. The way, your soul, the Universe, your intuition, your connection, your faith, your tribe, your ever-changing tools, your breath, your intention, all of it: that's the flow. Trust it.

The chaos breeds in all of our lives throughout all of our lives. Choosing joy isn't living in the absence of pain, it's being able to see between the web of static with faith that the air is clearer on the other side, and the confidence that if you hold on just long enough, you will once again fill your lungs with the sweet, crisp breeze and feel the sun warm your face.

Choose each other.
Choose love.
Choose your Self.
Choose joy.

And while you're at it, love fearlessly without the need to be loved back. Give freely to the world around you. Stay in that heart center. Your generosity feeds the cosmic fabric and disseminates positive change. Ultimately, the frequency you send out is that which will return to you in ways you could not have orchestrated yourself. Focus on the giving, not the getting. Receiving comes naturally and more poetically than you could ever have written it yourself.

I said it when we started: when the flow of life is disrupted, it's in our nature to close off. Our instinct is to contract when we should expand.

This is the time to dig deep, tap in, trust your connection to the Universe, and lead with your heart.

Let these 7 Secrets to survival help you remember how to shift from fear and uncertainty to peace and possibility. Remember your connection to yourself, the Universe, and each other. Remember the feeling of being whole, connected, joyful, and enough.

Trust your Self. Find your own joy even When Shit Goes Sideways.

Choosing joy doesn't mean there isn't pain. I want to be super clear here. Don't wait for life to smooth out before finding joy. Choose joy in the moments in between. Remember that the chaos is real.

If you find yourself looking at the woman who seems to have her shit together, check yourself and then look a little closer. Everyone has their own stuff that they are experiencing and working through. We all take steps backward on our path to move forward. The bumps and roadblocks along the way nudge you toward growth and allow you to be credible, trustworthy sources for others. There seems to be this universal belief that if I don't have all of my own issues sorted out, I can't possibly help others when my life is falling apart. To this, I call bullshit. And I have been on both sides, so trust me on this one.

Ever notice how the stuff that surfaces in your life tends to mirror what you're working on yourself or are helping a friend or client navigate? This is no coincidence. It's your teachers, the Universe, and your higher Self giving you opportunities to expand, to make choices, to reinforce beliefs in the exact moment you're committing to growth.

Lean in but take action. A mistake many people make, especially when shit is going sideways, is to rely solely on spiritual guidance. As I said, we are here on the plane of free will. You can receive inspired guidance, but you have to implement and take action.

As I write this now, I am facing some really big life stuff. Some days I wake up and wonder how I could possibly help other women when there are areas in which I am struggling. And then I work these seven secrets, and my blood pressure drops, my clarity expands, and my trust that the path will unfold just as it should is renewed. I sit with that for a minute and breathe. Then I remind myself to keep taking action.

Soul-centered navigation evolves as you do. Return to these pages when you need to remind yourself of your power and your connection. Set intention, move with love, leave the anger and resentment, and flow with your heart space.

It's no secret: You've got this.

Exercises & Reflections:

When life feels upended, when plates are spinning, trust that inside you have the tools to find the next step. You don't need the entire path lit. Keep carrying the torch to light the way and don't let the breeze from the spinning plates blow it out. Stay focused. Stay the course. Ask for help. Trust your Self.

The flicker of the torch will get you through the darkest days if you maintain hope and stay in the moment. What can you do right now to feed the torch's flame? In the moment of chaos, this is sometimes all you can wrap your head around. It's OK.

1) *Forget regret.* If you're currently struggling with regret and you've already addressed it or taken the action you can, then it's time to burn it up. Let go of those heavy feelings; unless they're a catalyst for change, holding on to them isn't doing anyone any good. Write any regrets on a piece of paper. Now hold that paper to your heart and fill yourself with gratitude. With each breathe you draw, feel gratitude fill your heart. Feel gratitude for the experiences and the opportunities for growth. Feel gratitude for yourself because it's time to forgive. When you're ready, lay the paper safely in a fire pit and watch as the fire burns the paper, the words, and the regrets and takes that energy back to the Universe for healing.

2) *Begin to create waves of change.* This is the start of choosing joy even if it's in pieces. Contemplating each of your Soul Centers, create a list of three ways you can begin to create positive change and momentum. These can be big sweeping waves or small ripples; it all helps build the shifts. This list should spark joy and hope.

3) *What will you allow yourself to tolerate as you navigate the murky waters?* As you think about your current situations, what will you allow yourself to tolerate before deciding to commit to the waves of change and for how long? For example, for 2 days, without self judgement, I will allow myself to sit in my jammies, eat ice cream, and binge watch Netflix. Then I'll be ready to launch waves of change.

4) *Give up control.* Remember, it is possible that you may not actually know the best outcome! What is it that you believe you want? Now, using your Soul Centers, journal how you think attaining that goal will make your *feel*? Spend some time on this because it's all in the feelings — that's where the flow feeds.

Now, start to focus more on the *feelings* that you're seeking and less on the outcomes. Raise your frequency to match that which you desire by dwelling in the feelings. Move forward and be more aware of opportunities to feel the way you want to feel. You'll be surprised to see many more options to get you where you want to be — which is to say, to get you to feel the way you want to feel. Journal your experiences to remind yourself that this process effectively shifts your frequency. Choose the joyful paths.

5) *Love unconditionally, even when things suck.* What three things can you do today to raise the frequency around you with love? Feeling committed to choosing joy? List three things for each Soul Center and then take action.

6) *What if it's less about them and more a lesson for you?* What mirrors are being held in front of you right now? Reviewing your Soul Centers, what is surfacing in your life right now? Jot these things down and ask yourself "what are these things/ issues/challenges/frustrations highlighting in your life and what lessons can they be teaching you?"

7) *It's all about finding and choosing Joy, even if it's in pieces.* Think automatic writing — anything goes, just write. For each Soul Center write down everything, no matter how large or small, that sparks joy. Fill your page; just keep the pen going. As you fill your page with flickers of joy, go back and circle all the pieces you currently have streaming in your life and really appreciate them. Feel the frequency of joy expand. Now, lean into the

idea that the others are on their way to you. This is the place to be, appreciating the bits you have and creating the frequency for the joy you're ready to feel.

8) *Rewrite the following:*

I trust my Self.
I am connected to my higher Self, the Universe, and others.
I am guided by my own purpose.
I mine my soul for solutions.
I am whole, connected, joyful, and enough.
I got this.

Join us for more support and community at JeanineTripodi.com/WSGS and join our Facebook group: When Sh*t Goes Sideways.

Jeanine Tripodi

ABOUT THE AUTHOR

Jeanine Tripodi is a Boston-born, Arizona-based speaker, author, and intuitive energetic healer. She is passionate about teaching others to remember their inner guidance system, trust their connection with the Universe, and learn to find joy within the chaos.

Through her intuitive energy sessions, one-on-one and small group mentorship, workshops, and retreats, she helps others lead lives through soul-centered navigation.

Jeanine is a Karuna Reiki™ Master Teacher and certified hypnotist.

Find out more about Jeanine at JeanineTripodi.com and follow her on instagram @JeanineTripodi.

NOTES

NOTES

Made in the USA
Columbia, SC
14 January 2020